Contents

This officer is an Empire Air Trainee and as such is considered to be already sufficiently decorated and is to receive no more regardless of further service.

Air Vice Marshal Sir George Jones

For Benjamin, Lauren, Ryan and Sam

Author's Note

As with my previous book, *Sidney Cotton: The Last Plane Out of Berlin*, this is the story of a fascinating man in a fascinating era—not a conventional biography, or a formal history. And as I said in that book, I have relied on the dramatic techniques of television, with some conversations and descriptions of events reconstructed.

But I have done research into the period—and also had the benefit of interviews with a number of people in the book, including Clive Caldwell himself. And of course I have had access to his personal papers—and for this I must thank Mrs Jean Caldwell for her generosity in this matter, and also to the staff of the Australian War Memorial, the National Library of Australia and National Archives of Australia for assistance and access to other material.

Introduction

Clive Caldwell would not have approved of this book, or for that matter any biography. He was approached many times by writers, but thwarted every attempt to set down the details of his extraordinary life.

This is not a conventional biography, and many conversations and events have been reconstructed. It is based on research into the man and conversations with his many admirers and some enemies.

In 1990, I asked him to lunch to try to get him to tell his story on television. He suggested that we meet at the Royal Automobile Club in Macquarie Street Sydney, one of his favourite haunts. While we were at the bar I tried to persuade him to take part in a debate with Air Marshal George Jones, his old enemy from the days of the Morotai Mutiny. What this involved, I patiently explained, was to go into a television studio and confront Jones.

'You'd have to put me into a cage first,' said Clive.

I had arrived at the club at 12.30, expecting to lunch at 1 pm—but at 2.30 he was still drinking, and I timidly enquired when we were going to eat.

'We've had our lunch,' said Clive, jabbing a finger at the empty whisky glasses.

Later he became strangely belligerent and glared at me as if he had never seen me before. He jabbed me in the chest with his finger and said: 'Are you recording this? I will sue you. Do you understand? I will sue you.'

I made limp attempts to persuade Clive Caldwell that there were no cameras or microphones present but he had ceased to listen. Later, when he was very ill I called him in hospital to give him my good wishes. He sounded frail and tired.

He said quite simply, 'Thank you very much. It is very kind of you.'

Like many others, I wish I had got to know him better.

Your head is throbbing from too many beers the night before and your first attempt to get your foot onto the wing fails; better have a pee up against the wheel of the plane; it's good luck and if we get frightened in combat we don't want any little accidents in the cockpit, do we?

The stick is cool to the touch and you pull it back into your stomach. God, it's cold. People don't believe you when you say its cold in the desert. You drag the clammy rubber oxygen mask over your mouth and turn on the oxygen. A few deep breaths and your head starts to clear. That's better. Pure oxygen. Just the thing for a hangover.

Now then, cockpit checks: set altimeter with the little winder on the side of the dial; we're only a hundred feet above sea level; grab the big handle on the floor, it's down there on the right hand side of the cockpit, and push it down—that opens the radiator shutters so the engine doesn't overheat while we're taxiing; work the twin piston hand pump up and down a few times to pressurise the hydraulic lines.

Master switch on, CLICK; fuel on, CLICK; tank selector switch to main fuel tank 55 gallons, CLICK; work the winding lever to adjust the rudder trim—it's a little black disc with white calibrations on it.

Two inches right for take-off; elevator to zero; throttle mixture to run idle rich—more fuel than air; check magnetos are both live; give the primer switch three or four flicks.

Put your head over the side and shout, clear prop.

The engine fires, runs backwards against compression then fires again. Black smoke from the fish-tail shaped exhaust pipes, six on each side. One by one other Tomahawks explode into life around you and the backwash from the propeller throws up a sandstorm. Can't see a bloody thing because of the sand on the windscreen.

Wave to one of the erks to wipe the screen.

Clear for take-off. Your head is clear but there is a lead weight in your stomach. You feel like you want to throw up.

So is this going to be the day I don't return?

The ace

He had killed a thousand men either in the air or on the ground and now he was to be found at the end of the bar. Not sitting down—that would have signified defeat—but standing straight and tall, holding court, staring people out with a gaze like a laser beam. Many people took one look and avoided him.

It was not that he was old—on the contrary Clive Caldwell held his age well. But there was something about Clive. He dominated the room—sometimes he was bigger than the room—even when he was glowing with whisky.

Many men were afraid of him. Caldwell looked at men and assessed them and most did not pass the test. In truth, he *did* want to talk about what he had done in the air force, but there were not too many people who would listen any more. He could be abrasive and obdurate until you got to know him.

His story was about World War II, but there had been a lot of wars since then. Korea, Vietnam, the Gulf Wars and many other actions. Clive Caldwell did not want to cover himself in glory, but he did like to set the record straight.

Sooner or later, he would find his way to the lift and, carefully drive home in his old Mercedes.

Just another cranky old bastard who had done something in the war.

Well, quite a lot, actually.

Ace /eis/n. a single spot or mark on a card or die; a playing card marked with a single spot; in tennis a serve which the opponent fails to touch; a very small quantity, amount or degree; a particle; *within an ace of winning*; a highly skilled person; an adept: *an ace at tap dancing; Brit.*, a fighter pilot credited by the RAF with shooting down five or more enemy aeroplanes.

Soldiers fighting on the ground do not usually talk about the number of men they have killed, neither do sailors. There are no aces in the army or the navy, no count of tanks destroyed, or ships sunk.

Fighter pilots are uneasy on that score, and maintain that shooting down an aircraft will not necessarily result in the death of the man flying it, although it often does. It isn't something that is openly discussed.

The concept of an ace has been around since men first fitted guns to aeroplanes, but has never been officially recognised. An ace is a pilot who has destroyed in air-to-air combat at least five aircraft or shares with others the destruction of such a number of aircraft. So, a pilot may have destroyed four aircraft and share with another pilot the destruction of another two. Those two *halves* are then counted as one aircraft destroyed. So he becomes an ace.

Clive Caldwell lies tenth in a list of British and Commonwealth fighter pilots in World War II. Ahead of him are two South Africans, four Englishmen, a Frenchman, an Irishman and a Canadian.

He keeps distinguished company: Pat Pattle and Sailor Malan (South Africans), Pierre Clostermann (French) and Paddy Finucane (Irish), Johnny Johnson, Neville Duke, Bob Braham and Bob Stanford-Tuck (English), George Beurling (Canadian). They were sailors and estate agents, expert knife throwers, rowing blues, sheep farmers and bankers.

A little more than one thousand Allied pilots became aces in World War II. More than a third of those died during the war, and those who survived are in their eighties or nineties.

Of the top ten pilots, only Neville Duke survives (in early 2005). He is 83 years old, lives in England, and still owns and flies a private plane.

The top scoring Allied pilot of the war was Pat Pattle, who officially shot down 41 aircraft, but many people believe his score could be as high as 60.

Caldwell's score is ahead of many more high profile pilots—like Douglas Bader (23) of *Reach For The Sky* fame, who fought the war with two artificial legs; Al Deere (22) the New Zealander who became aide-de-camp to Her Majesty the Queen; Bluey Truscott (17) a fellow Australian who died in a flying accident during the war; Peter Townsend (11) who squired Princess Margaret, and another Australian, Richard Hillary (5), author of *The Last Enemy*, whose handsome face suffered terrible burns in a blazing Spitfire.

Clive's score is usually listed as 28 and a half, although some historians have maintained that he took part in 30 kills— 27 plus three shared. To this must be added six probables and fifteen damaged. In the heat of battle it is easy to make mistakes. Several pilots would often have claimed in good faith to have destroyed the same aircraft so any score is open to dispute. And witnesses are often hard to find.

But the Germans he flew against racked up much bigger scores. In the North African desert Clive's old enemies, Hans-Joachim Marseille, maintained that he shot down 158 aircraft; and Werner Schroer—who claimed Clive as a kill—114.

In Russia, the Germans shot down scores of inferior Soviet aeroplanes, many of them made of wood. Erich Hartmann claimed to have destroyed 352 Yaks, Ilyushins and Migs, Gerhard Barkhorn, 301 and Gunther Rall, 275. If Caldwell had flown against the Russians, one wonders what his score would have been.

If there were two aeroplanes that produced aces, they were the Spitfire and the Messerschmitt. Of the five Allied pilots with scores larger than 30, four gained their victories in the Spitfire. Likewise the Me-109 was the type flown most by German aces.

Twenty of Clive Caldwell's combat successes were in North Africa, and in all of them he was flying an aircraft which both the British and the Germans considered to be inferior to both the Spitfire and the Messerschmitt. That aircraft was the P 40 either in its Tomahawk or Kittyhawk versions.

As one American general said, it was an aeroplane that was damned by words but flown to glory.

Shooting the clock

The life of a trainee bank clerk could not by any definition be described as exciting, but the young Clive Caldwell had very little say in his career path—it had been decided for him by his father.

Clive's first job after leaving school was behind the counter at the Bank of New South Wales. He wore a dark suit and a white starched collar. Everything that happened in a working day was governed by the large, wooden-framed clock that hung on the wall. Next to it was a calendar. It was Clive's job to wind the clock and change the calendar.

At 10 o'clock every morning the bank opened; not a minute before and not a minute after. At closing time, 3 pm, the routine was repeated. Clive grew to hate that clock. Its sonorous ticking represented his life ebbing away

In 1929 there were no ATMs or credit cards. If you did

not make it to the bank at closing time on Friday, it could be a bleak weekend.

It was Clive's job to shut the doors and ignore the cries of those who had left their visit a little too late. The manager would produce a fob watch from his waistcoat pocket, and count down the seconds: 'Caldwell, will you please close the doors? And when you have done that, back to the ledger.'

After the door was closed it became airless in the bank. The columns of red and blue numbers swam before his eyes, and the stiff collar chafed his neck. Clive glanced at the hands of the clock but they scarcely seem to have moved at all. Another two hours before he could go home.

Like all the tellers, Clive had been issued with a small revolver in a drawer beneath the counter. This was supposed to offer some kind of protection in the event of a bank robbery. Unlike his colleagues, Clive was used to handling guns, and was an excellent shot. The bank maintained a shooting gallery in the cellar, and Clive regularly practised there. During the quiet periods he would take the gun out of the drawer and handle it, feeling the weight in his hand.

Tick, tick, tick went the big clock.

Clive felt a pulse pounding in his temples, and a red mist film slipped down further into his field of vision. A bank was no place for a man of action.

He drew the pistol from the drawer and fired twice at the big clock. The first shot shattered the glass. The second made a neat hole in the clock face. Then the entire clock fell off the wall. Shards of glass tinkled on the parquet floor, and bits of clock spring and gear wheels performed a crazy pirouette. One of the female tellers gave a little scream.

Clive Caldwell's career with the bank was over. And he had had scored his first kill.

Planes for pig iron

At the outbreak of World War II, the Royal Australian Air Force had no modern aeroplanes. The RAAF had 310 officers and 3179 airmen, but its aeroplanes should have been in a museum. Most of its 264 aircraft were obsolete types which did not look that much different from those of the Great War.

Almost all of them were British.

The frontline fighter was the Hawker Demon, a biplane which had first flown in 1933. The Demon had only half the speed of the new monoplane fighters appearing in Britain and Germany, and by 1939 had been relegated to a training role.

Slightly more modern was the Avro Anson of 1935. This at least looked a bit more contemporary. It was a modern, low-wing machine with two engines and wheels tucked up under them. It was not a high-performance machine, but a practical workaday aircraft which could be used for coastal surveillance, training or as a bomber. But it did not look especially threatening. Also entering service was the Wirra-way, a locally produced aircraft that had been intended as an advanced trainer, but which was now, very optimistically, to be pressed into service as a fighter bomber.

Australia had traditionally bought British aircraft but the British aircraft industry could not deliver. In 1940 it was fully committed to producing machines for the Royal Air Force and the war in Europe. Australia turned towards Japan.

On 19 February 1942, just 74 days after the attack on Pearl Harbor, the port of Darwin was attacked by the Imperial Japanese Navy. The aeroplanes used were a mixture of fighters, bombers and torpedo carriers—the Mitsubishi A 6M Zero, the Mitsubishi G 4M Betty and the Nakajima Kate.

Between the two World Wars the Australian government had continued to hold to its position that war happened else-where, that Australia would never have to defend itself, and only needed to be prepared in case it needed to assist Britain. It was silently assumed that Britain, of course, would quickly jump to this country's defence in the unlikely, even un-imaginable event of any attack on Australia. Few were of the opinion that a strong, independent and expensive defence force was needed. The prevailing attitude was that Australia only needed to be able to help out to the best of the capabilities of a small country, if and when the time arose.

There had been little or no attempt to obtain modern fighting planes for the RAAF, and almost nothing done to support local design and manufacture until the Common-wealth Aircraft Corporation was formed in the mid-1930s.

Throughout the 1930s cables went back and forth between Australia and Britain about RAAF aircraft requirements, becoming more urgent as the threat of a second European war became apparent.

At the Imperial Conference in 1937, Australia had expressed its concern about the long delays in obtaining orders from British manufacturers. The delegation had argued that the requirements of the dominions should be given priority over foreign countries. As the (British) Air Ministry dictated to, and controlled, aircraft manufacturers, it should have been able to insist that ordinary commercial orders would not take precedence—which would result in Australia's orders not being filled promptly.

Other trading partners had been canvassed. During the 1930s Australia and Japan were engaged in useful trade, and several large Japanese trading companies had local offices in various Australian cities, buying Australian primary produce and promoting Japanese manufactured goods in return.

Many agreeable contracts were being signed. Some of Australia's wool exported to Japan came back as cloth or clothing. Deals were considered to exchange raw product from Australia for ships built in Japan. Large orders for wool were placed to supply manufacturers of the uniforms for the Japanese defence forces. The trading partnership was developing very well overall.

A curious fact was that barely a year before Japan's attack on Pearl Harbor, Australia had tried to place an order for Japanese combat aircraft. In November 1940 Australia was at war with Germany, but relations with Japan were still cordial. As a token of friendship, Emperor Hirohito had even made a gift of flowering cherry trees to be planted in Canberra.

One of the major Japanese companies with offices in Australia was Mitsubishi Shoji Kaisha Ltd, manufacturers of the Zero and the Betty bomber.

Sir John Latham, head of Australia's diplomatic mission to Japan, knew that Britain was not in a position to supply aircraft to Australia. He had lived in Japan for two years and was only too aware of the astonishing strides that had been made in the production of war matériel. Latham believed that Britain and Australia could not oppose Japanese expansion in Asia, and that it was better to keep the Japanese on side with trade and shipping deals.

Not all Australians felt the same. In 1938, Prime Minister Joe Lyons had banned iron ore exports to Japan, believing that Australia's reserves should be preserved. In Port Kembla, waterside workers had refused to load ships with pig iron for Japan because of Japan's invasion of China. Robert Menzies, then Attorney-General, sided with Latham and forced the workers to load the ships earning for himself the eternal sobriquet 'Pig Iron Bob'. Menzies wanted to appease Japan, and to continue trading with it, while seeking to interest the United States in Australia's defence if push came to shove.

Mitsubishi was keen to clinch the deal but, as far as the Australian government was concerned, the planes were only a stop-gap until British or American types could be acquired. The RAAF was primarily interested in a twin-engined training aircraft similar to the Anson, but enquiries were also made about the immediate delivery of current fighter types like the Zero.

The total value of the 40 aircraft was £500 000, with the price per aircraft £12 500. They were to be paid for, wrote John McEwen, not with cash but with pig iron:

> . . . by counter supply to Japan not in cash but in products, e.g. platinum, pig iron, scrap iron, molybdenum, nickel, aluminium, lead, cobalt, zinc, etc, the company stating that if any of these supplies are not produced or available in Australia Japan would be extremely pleased if, with Commonwealth intermediation, they could be supplied from, say Canada.

If the deal had been signed in November 1940, the aircraft would all have been delivered to Australia within 20 months. It never happened, but some of the aircraft arrived anyway . . . in the skies above Darwin on 19 February 1942.

Clive Caldwell would probably have given one of his wry smiles at the thought of Zeros in Australian colours! And in a contest between Japanese and Australian Zeros, who would have been the winner?

A born leader and a first class shot

In November 1987 at the age of 77, Clive Caldwell wrote about the pilots who had served under him in World War II:

> What I think is required of our operational fighter pilots is not just a cool head, cold heart and quick reflexes as is supposedly the case. A cool head certainly, quick reflexes of course and a resolute heart with a rich red coloured liver to go with it.
>
> The kind of nerves that can recognise the odds and having assessed the situation can commit himself totally to strike the destroying blow without regard to survival which is always a welcome bonus but never a prerequisite.
>
> It is this kind of integrity of purpose that allowed such men as those to face such occasions time and time again

until they either die in doing it or come through to the end. And for all this they were paid in pennies and tin medals. The pennies—taxed if a way could be found—and often the medals were withheld while their own people safe at home denied them the acclaim they so richly deserved.

And yet some of the survivors are still willing to appear before the public on Anzac Day not for public acclaim but for themselves, to remember together those days when they feared no man—and damn few women.

Towards the end of World War II a number of Australia's most distinguished fighter pilots became so disillusioned with the way the war in the Pacific was being conducted that they resigned their commissions. This was an unthinkable act in times of war, tantamount to an act of treason. In earlier wars, men had been shot for less. The episode happened in a place called Morotai in the Dutch East Indies and became known as the Morotai Mutiny. The officers included Caldwell, Australia's highest scoring pilot of the World War II.

Clive Caldwell looked like a Hollywood actor: tall and good looking, he was a brilliant pilot, an excellent marksman and a born leader of men. He flew Spitfires and Kittyhawks in Europe, North Africa and the South-West Pacific. He fought the Germans, the Italians, the Vichy French and the Japanese, and shot down at least 30 enemy aircraft. The Morotai Mutiny revealed a festering sore that was the conflict between permanent officers in the Royal Australian Air Force—many of whom had never flown an aeroplane and never would—and enlisted men, clerks, roustabouts and adventurers who had offered their services to fight for their country.

Most of the Australian pilots who fought in World War II did so a long way from home. When they returned to Australia they expected to be treated as heroes but they were not. It appeared there were two sorts of Air Force officer— those who sat behind desks at the Defence Department in Melbourne and those who steered an exotic dangerous machine over deserts and jungles. The career officers were the *shiny bum brigade*. The fighter pilots were the *glamour boys*.

Clive Robertson Caldwell was born in Sydney on 28 July 1910.

Nothing much else of note happened on that day. There was a revolution in Portugal and a war in Honduras. But in Canada the politician Sir Wilfred Laurier made a patriotic speech exalting the virtues of the British Empire:

> We believe that our form of government, that is the monarchical form of government presided over by the Royal Family in England, we have a King and Queen in which we have a right to be proud and of this constitution, we say that it is the best in any community that has ever existed.

One of the obligations of being a member of that Empire, said Sir Wilfred was defending it, a duty that Clive Caldwell would later discharge admirably.

In 1910 the Australia that Clive Caldwell was born into was very much a part of that Empire. The playboy King, Edward VII had died on 6 May that year, and had been succeeded by his eldest son George V. George was a popular monarch who, as the Duke of York, had attended the ceremony of Federation in Australia nine years before. Like Clive Caldwell he was a good shot; indeed, reckoned by many to be the best shot in England.

Aeroplanes were to play a large part in Clive Caldwell's life, but in 1910 they scarcely existed. Aeroplanes were an amusing distraction, dangerous things, a flash in the pan. The people went back to the daily grind. The politicians droned on about the drought; the dull clerks returned to their dull ledgers. Australians went back to sleep. Maybe some of the more imaginative reflected on what they had seen.

Just twelve days before Clive was born a man called John Duigan had made the first flight in an Australian-designed aircraft at Spring Plains in Victoria. But it would be another three years before Australia set up its own air force. The Australian Flying Corps was formed at Point Cook in Victoria in 1913.

Clive was born into a middle class family. His father Jack was bank manager of the English Scottish and Australian Bank in Darling Street, Rozelle, an inner suburb of Sydney. His mother Annie died when Clive was quite young.

He went to school at Trinity Grammar School and Sydney Grammar School. Although he always said his academic record was unremarkable, he had won the English prize. In sport, however, he showed great ability. He was stroke of the first four in the head of the river regatta, and after leaving school became the state junior javelin champion. In 1930 and

1932 he represented New South Wales in the Australian amateur track and field championships.

Bruce Watson who was later to fly with him in the RAAF knew of his sporting ability but had never actually met him: 'In the 400 metres race the only part of him I ever saw was his backside. He was much faster than me.'

Clive was good with his fists too. Money was tight so to make a little ready cash Clive would occasionally fight in bouts at the Rushcutters Bay Stadium and come away with £5 in cash—a tidy sum in the 1930s.

When he was hit on the nose he concealed his injuries from his father by stuffing tissue paper up each nostril. It was his habit to fight under an assumed name and occasionally he sparred with boxing greats like the Aboriginal boxer Ron Richards, who later became Australian middleweight champion.

The two were evenly matched and became good friends. Rather than fight aggressively, they usually would only spar. But one day, while fighting a bout, Clive noticed a change in Richards:

There was a viciousness about him that I'd never experienced before. But this day I realised he was determined. So I became just as determined. I think I gave as good as I received, but I had taken a few pretty nasty punches earlier which shook me a bit.

Then I found out afterwards that someone said to Richards before he stepped into the ring, 'This is the fellow that called you an Aboriginal black bastard'.

It transpired that there was money on the fight and the punter wanted to see Richards provoked. Clive would never have said anything of the sort and the two remained close friends until Richards died in 1967.

•

Twelve thousand miles away in Europe Hitler had embarked on his goal of world domination. Clive decided that that was where he wanted to be.

Like most boys Clive idolised the fighter pilots of World War I—Albert Ball, Billy Bishop, Raymond Collishaw; and the Germans Ernst Udet, Max Immelmann and, of course, Manfred Von Richthofen. As a teenager he befriended Andrew King Cowper, who had been born in Bellevue Hill in Sydney, and who had accounted for nineteen German aircraft in combat over the fields of Flanders.

> I could picture myself there rolling though the clouds shooting them down and becoming a fighter ace! Later on during World War II, I came to know Raymond Collishaw, Arthur Coningham, Billy Bishop, Cole, Wally Hammond and Harry Cobby pretty well.

In 1938 Clive joined the Royal Aero Club of New South Wales at Mascot aerodrome where he befriended the flying instructor Bob Wingrove. 'Whenever he was short of a few bob he would sell me a half hour lesson,' recalled Clive in an interview later in life.

Clive soloed after only three and a half hours of instruction and, by the outbreak of war, had just over eleven hours of flying time on Tiger Moths.

What with the boxing and the athletics and the flying lessons, women did not play a large part in Clive's formative years. If he went out, it was usually with a group of boys and girls. Clive preferred outdoor activities rather than the theatre or the cinema. Often the gang used to go ice skating at the Glaciarium or the Palais. Among them was a quietly composed young woman from country New South Wales.

Jean McIver grew up on the family wheat property, 'Retreat', at Illabo, close to Cootamundra and near the soldier settlement of Dirnaseer. She boarded at Ascham school in Sydney, and met Clive through a schoolfriend. When Jean left school she took up nursing, learning her craft at the Wootton private hospital in Kings Cross in Sydney.

After his premature departure from the bank, Clive took a number of jobs. He seemed to have no particular career in mind. He went jackarooing in Queensland; he ran a garage in Darlinghurst with a man called Jim Doyle and later worked in the MLC insurance office.

Clive and Jean were married on 13 April 1940, at the little church on Jean's family property at Illabo.

•

At the outbreak of war in September 1939, Clive found himself with a little problem. He wanted to be a fighter pilot, but he was three years over the maximum age of 28 for RAAF fighter training. 'It was darned near too late for me. I was three years too old for single seater training so I had to have my birth certificate very expertly altered. That got me in.'

Clive fronted up to the recruiting centre in Erskine Street near Wynyard station. The corporal who received him was a keen follower of athletics and instantly recognised him because of his success on the sports field. 'Anyway this corporal looked at my certificate and then he looked up at me and said, "I know you—you're a lot older than it says here".'

Clive was thinking on his feet and replied: 'No, you're getting me confused with my older brother, B C Caldwell. I'm C R Caldwell and he's three years older than me. We both went to Grammar, and I think you've got the two of us mixed up.'

The corporal was suspicious. 'I think there's something fishy going on here,' he said, tapping his pencil on the desk.

Clive waded in like a prize fighter, the famous rasping voice the unblinking stare. 'You have no right to challenge me and you have no right to cross examine me. I have complied with the request to produce my birth certificate and that is what I have done.'

There was a pause. The corporal fumbled in his desk and produced a rubber stamp and waved it uncertainly above the form. He brought it down heavily on the document and scribbled something in the margin with his pencil. Bugger it, he said under his breath.

Clive waited until he was outside the recruiting office before he shook his head and allowed himself a snort of laughter.

So, as far as the Royal Australian Air Force was concerned, Clive Caldwell was not born in 1910, but three years later on 28 July 1913. Many pilots lied about their ages to get into the service but usually to make themselves older. Clive was now officially 26 again. To his fellow fighter pilots he always *seemed* older, almost a father figure.

Clive had presented the phoney certificate to the RAAF in September 1939, but had to wait until February 1940 for his call up papers. To his dismay, he discovered that all the men on his course were to be trained as instructors. This was not what Clive had in mind; he had set his heart on becoming a fighter pilot, not taking rookies on circuits and bumps. So he discharged himself, hoping to be accepted on a future course where, with luck, he would be posted overseas.

Why did he want to go to war?

It was the thing to do of course. An impulse adventure. There was a great game to be played in which I wanted to take part to see how I would go when the whips started cracking. Anyway war is the male's second favourite activity or so it seems. Also I was irritated by that ranting little bastard Hitler and his mob of the self-styled master race. There was an urge to feel the satisfaction of being able to spit in the face of such arrogance. In any case one does what one has to even if it's only paid in pennies and tin medals.

Clive entered the RAAF for the second time on 25 April 1940 as an AC-2 aircrew trainee and a member of No 1 Course Empire Air Training Scheme. Even at this early stage of his career in the service, there was an incident which highlighted the animosity shown by RAAF regular officers towards civilians who had joined up to fight for King and Country.

At Wagga Wagga, the men on his course were addressed by an RAAF regular officer, Group Captain Bull Garing, who did not mince his words. He said: 'You are known as Empire Air Scheme but so far as I am concerned you are Empire Air Scum.'

To a proud man like Caldwell this was deeply insulting, and it set the pattern for years of ongoing friction between him and the RAAF hierarchy.

Dick Cresswell was an instructor at Wagga, training pilots to fly the Australian-built CAC Wirraway, a two-seat advanced trainer built in Melbourne. Caldwell was in one of his two flights.

One day he sent Clive on a navigation exercise from Wagga to Cootamundra, Narrandera, and then back to Wagga. Instead of doing the complete course, Clive flew the Wirraway to Illabo to see Jean. As Cresswell said:

> I caught him out. He used to land in a wheatfield, take out sufficient fuel as if he'd done the rest of the cross country, write up his log perfectly and fly straight back to Wagga. Stuck the spare petrol in a drum and put it in his car, I guess. A one and a half hour flight. Others came back with a perfect navigational record.

Cresswell was suspicious when he took a look at Clive's logbook. It is not easy to write notes in a vibrating aircraft, but Clive's handwriting was unusually neat. Unless, of course, he had written the notes while on the ground at Illabo?

There was no doubt that Clive was a competent pilot, but one of his commanding officers thought that he was apt to let his keenness get the better of him. 'He needs more practice in leading and will turn out a very good pilot. At the moment he is purely an individualist.'

Clive had hoped to be sent to England to fight in the Battle of Britain, but that was all over by October 1940. The RAF was now moving over to the offensive, with fighter sweeps over occupied France, but Clive missed out on those too.

Commissioned as a pilot officer, it was not until February 1941 that he embarked for the Middle East. Six weeks after arriving in Egypt he joined 250 Squadron, Royal Air Force at Aquir in Palestine.

The western desert

S and.
   Sand in your eyes. Sand in your ears. Sand up your nose. Sand in the bully beef. Sand in the engine of your aeroplane. And flies. Millions of flies. They settled on your food, flew into your mouth and nibbled on the desert sores on your arms and legs.

Unlike the British, the Australians were used to the flies. Those who had worked as jackeroos like Caldwell were used to sleeping rough on the ground in the clothes they stood up in. But a man could die of thirst in this awful place. Only the Berbers seemed to have any idea how to live here. They would wander through the battlefield with their camels and veiled women without taking much interest in any of it.

There was never enough to drink. Water was rationed to a gallon a day for each man and every drop was precious. Water used for washing or shaving was used to top up the radiators of vehicles.

In these harsh conditions the sand got into everything; millions of tiny particles were swept along by the wind. If sand was sucked into the air intake of an aero engine it could mingle with the lubricating oil, forming a harsh abrasive and turn machinery into a piece of scrap within hours. The engineers had to strain the petrol through chamois filters to try to keep the dirt and dust out of the fuel.

To stop getting sand in the engine, ugly looking air filters were fitted under the snouts of the the aircraft, but in the air these slowed the aeroplanes down. And they spoiled the clean lines of the Spitfire.

The food was dreary and repetitious; bully beef and biscuits. Fresh milk, fresh vegetables and fruit were like gold. Occasionally one of the men would shoot a gazelle which made a welcome change, but it was tough and gamey and not to everyone's taste. Because of the lack of vitamin C, many men soon acquired desert sores. Like eighteenth century sailors, they were candidates for scurvy, and worse.

The airfields were like no airfields Caldwell had ever seen before—just patches of desert cleared of rocks fringed with tents and caravans. It was as if a circus had just arrived in town but this circus was full of bad tempered, ill-shaven men who lived without women. And he wrote about it all.

Tomorrow, this indifferent Pole or Jem the quiet man or old MacWilliams or myself would cross over into the ranks of the newly dead, and join the countless numbers of those who had once watched the sun setting in a flash of green light at the rim of the desert and found even the smell of fried bully beef acceptable. It began to seem as if I was condemned to wander around the world engaged in a futile war until a bullet or a crash singled me out and gave me the answer to all the questions asked since childhood.

We quarrel among ourselves until one of our number is attacked by someone outside the circle. Afterwards, if they survive, they persuade themselves that they share the glory with the high commanders who get the knighthoods and the public acclaim. The abysmal folly of it all. We gather together half a million men, equip them at a fabulous cost, transport them God knows how many thousands of miles then engage in a death struggle with total strangers for causes that remain obscure. At the end of it what do we do? Break our promises to the survivors whom a grateful nation . . . will not need again.

The survivors of real operations can sit for hours, memories making light of physical discomfort. They are good memories. We never remember the bad times except in our dreams.

At night in the desert and Clive Caldwell wrote in his small black notebook:

The personal experiences related in the pages that follow may not be without interest. If it were possible, I should like to give a background to the story of my 19 months as a fighter pilot in the Middle East; but I realise that nothing

I could say would give the reader who has never been in the desert, or who has never known the process of killing-fighting, a true picture of the men I knew and served with.

Scenery of course can be described and readers with imagination can picture for themselves the vast space and everlasting nothingness that is Egypt and Libya. Human actions and motives are what is difficult to interpret. Readers of such matters inevitably think how they would act in similar circumstances and apply to others motives by which they would have been influenced.

It was a pity, Clive reflected, that the war had to come to a place as beautiful as Mersa Matruh.

Of all the places in the desert where imagination creates satisfying dreams, Mersa Matruh cannot be surpassed. Reflected in opalescent turquoise blue lagoons you see the sad remains of Cleopatra's once magnificent summer palace. You see purple sailed galleys float past in your imagination.

Mersa Matruh was an ancient port to which the Greeks brought their finest wares, armour, shields and works of art to barter for Ethiopian gold from across the Libyan desert, also slaves, gold, ivory and precious stones.

Clive was fascinated with the history of the place. Three thousand years earlier Queen Cleopatra *had* come here to relax and swim in the lagoon.

Mersa Matruh's star had dimmed a little by the 1930s, but

this was still one of the jewels of the Mediterranean, a popular retreat for the rich and famous. King Farouk of Egypt vacationed in Mersa Matruh to escape the swirling grit and humidity of Cairo. The Duke and Duchess of Windsor had stayed at the famous pink hotel and drunk daiquiris on the terrace, Wallis looking elegant in a gown by Schiaparelli.

This lovely seaside town had been shot to pieces by the time Clive saw it but it was still charming in the sunshine. The pink hotel at Mersa Matruh was only a shell, and the whole coast wore a ravaged air. There was rubble where the villages had been and the road was battered and sunk and littered with wrecked vehicles.

The townspeople had fled.

A mosquito settled on Clive's arm and bit. In his medical kit was some ammonia in a small bottle. He rubbed some onto the wound. Tomorrow, he thought grimly, it is possible that a very big mosquito will bite him.

Sitting outside my tent in the cool air in the intense peace of the starlit sky surrounded by the deep quiet of the desert it was difficult to realise the passions and prejudices which developed hate in men's hearts and drove them to destroy each other.

And then with the dusk comes the shadowed promise of the desert night. The stars appear like brilliant lamps and it is lighter again. There is a mysterious warmth, a feeling that seems to draw you close and make you part of the heart and pulse of the desert. Not bad for a boy from Sydney Grammar School.

There was great excitement in the squadron, the first to be equipped with the new American P 40C Tomahawk fighter.It had a maximum speed of 345 mph (555 km/h) and range of 800 miles (1287 km) and was armed with two .50 machine guns in the nose and four .30 machine guns in the wings.

Although he was to fly more modern and sophisticated aircraft, this was the machine in which Clive was to score 20 of his 28 victories.

A sharp axe: the Tomahawk

My introduction to the Tomahawk P 40 was on being posted to the newly formed No 250 Squadron RAF, the first in the Middle East to be equipped with these aircraft at the end of 1941, and I remained with them until I was posted in December to command 112 Squadron RAF then equipping with the Kittyhawk. Of the two (Tomahawk and Kittyhawk) I preferred the Tomahawk as a pilot's aircraft favouring only the greater lethal density of the Kittyhawks six .50 guns. Although later on in the UK, North-West Pacific and South-West Pacific area I flew much better performing aircraft, the Tomahawks were the best the RAF had in the Middle East and I was glad to be flying them. I liked their flush-riveted clean lines and the aeroplane itself.

They were wanting in performance, but the Allison engine was honest, hard working and reliable. The fuel injection which kept it running smoothly in all attitudes was a very good feature. The aeroplane handled and turned well, gave a fair warning of the stall, recovered from a spin without fuss and in general had little vice. In service they proved strong and rugged, and would stand up to a lot of punishment from opposing fire as well as violent aerobatics. They picked up speed quickly in a dive, but at steep angles of dive at high speed considerable strength of arm and leg and/or a lot of activity with the trim gear were needed to keep control.

The armament was adequate. The two .50 guns firing through the airscrew (omitted on the later Kittyhawks) were especially useful at close range; the .30 wing guns were changed over to .303s to take advantage of the more sophisticated ammunition available for these guns.

The Tomahawk, according to Clive, did have one serious fault:

The cockpit canopy when jettisoned from the near closed or well forward position swung inwards through the cockpit striking the pilot a heavy blow on the face or head. My own experience with this . . . from which I was very lucky to recover in time, brought this to light with consequent appropriate warning to the pilots.

It is greatly to the aircraft's credit that it stood up to the work so well in the desert and especially of the ground staff for the high degree of serviceability they achieved under the conditions for maintenance, often seemingly impossible and never less than difficult, in which the Desert Air Force operated.

Early in 1942, Caldwell left 250 Squadron to take command of 112 Squadron which, like other P 40 squadrons, were converting to the upgraded P 40 Kittyhawks moving through Kittyhawk IIIs and IVs as the war progressed. But the truth was the Germans aeroplanes were better.

In North Africa Clive met a tall blonde Englishman called Neville Duke. Duke was later to achieve fame as a test pilot for the Hawker company. Duke and Caldwell both liked the Tomahawk.

The Tomahawk was a lovely aeroplane to fly; it was beautifully built but it was a bit underpowered, . . . too well built for operational use with the power it had. It didn't have the climb or the altitude performance of the Spitfire but it was a good gun platform with two .50s in the nose and four 303s.

The gun breeches protruded into the cockpit so if you had a jam you could clear it.

You got the lovely smell of cordite when it fired. But you cleared it with the breech blocks. The Tomahawk was ideal for the rough landing grounds we had at that time. Very robust. Took a lot of punishment as well. A lot of them came back with bits missing. They had holes all over the place but they still flew.

•

It is not commonly known that Australians killed a great number of Frenchmen in World War II.

Before flying in combat against the Luftwaffe, Caldwell

was in action against the Vichy French in Syria. This was a nasty little sideshow to the war in which Australians were involved on the ground and in the air. It lasted barely a month, but the French strongly resisted the Allied invasion, and about 500 Australians died in the conflict.

Most of the time the Tomahawks were engaged in escorting Blenheim bombers but occasionally they took part in strafing attacks against French airfields. On 12 May 1942, Clive's logbook records that he escorted the bombers to Palmyra (now Tadmor) in Syria; one enemy aircraft was damaged and one was set on fire on the ground.

The French had carelessly left their aircraft in neat rows rather than disperse them in pens around the airfield. This made them extremely vulnerable to attack from the air, although the attacking aircraft were equally at risk from anti-aircraft fire. The Tomahawks had taken off at first light and were over the airfield by breakfast time. They swept in at a low level formation with Clive in the lead.

Clive was just about to fire his guns when, to his astonishment, he saw two French pilots leaning on the wing of a Morane fighter, entertaining two pretty girls. He was low enough to see a bottle of champagne resting on the leading edge of the wing and the girls were sipping from champagne glasses. He took his finger off the gun button and pulled the aircraft up in a steep climb.

'A late night or an early breakfast?' he thought. 'Anyway I don't shoot girls in frocks.'

By the time he came in for the second attack the pilots and girls had scattered, although Clive hoped they were not hiding under the wings. The anti-aircraft gunners had been taken by surprise on the first pass, but now they had his range and speed and it would not do to hang around too long.

Clive's logbook reports, 'One enemy aircraft damaged, one enemy aircraft on fire on the ground'. Over the next few days fellow Australians in the RAAF's 3 Squadron scored notable victories in the air against French fighters, six being shot down over Palmyra. Clive however had yet to make his first kill.

Some people say they shot down enemy planes on their first or second missions. I find those stories hard to believe. For the first few times I went up I didn't have much of a clue of what was going on. It took me thirty missions to bag my first kill.

They didn't seem to notice me and I began to feel a bit neglected. I had been hit one or two times and I didn't enjoy being on the receiving end.

After the exhausted French surrendered in Syria, Clive was sent to do temporary duty on the island of Cyprus, but this was to prove the lull before the storm. In June 1941, 250 Squadron moved forward from Alexandria to Sidi Haneish to provide air cover over the battlefield.

The Allies had decimated the Italian army but they now had Field Marshal Erwin Rommel to contend with. As the Germans consolidated their position the fighter squadrons changed their technique to ground strafing.

Clive wrote: 'There is a detached feeling in sitting in an aircraft firing at a man on the ground. The man below has no reality as a human being. He is just a target and it's your sole purpose to knock him over.'

Thirty-three sorties came and went, and there were still no victories in the air. Clive notes that his first confirmed kill was a Me-109. But it now seems likely that he shared in the destruction of an Italian Cant Z 1007 bomber near Alexandria on 8 June 1942. This was originally solely credited to a Flying Officer Hamlyn over Alexandria, the first victory claimed over Egypt by a Tomahawk.

The Cant was a large three-engined torpedo bomber built entirely of wood by the aviation division of a famous Italian naval construction firm based in Trieste.

Shooting shadows

Any duck hunter is familiar with the technique of aiming off—firing not at the moving bird but ahead of it so that the bullets and the target arrive at the same place at the same time and the bird flies into the shot.

In World War II, very few pilots survived long enough in battle to master the art of aiming off or, as it was correctly known, deflection shooting.

The solution was a device which would do the job for them. It was called the gyro gunsight or GGS. This consisted of a rapidly spinning mirror mounted on a universal joint connecting it to a hemisphere of thin copper rotating between the two poles of powerful magnets. This enabled the pilot to fly his aircraft so that an illuminated ring was centred on the target, the lead angle and even the gravity drop of the bullets being allowed for.

In combat the pilot would aim at the target and swivel the

handle of his throttle like a motor cyclist. This would cause the ring to expand or contract. When the ring encased the wing span of the enemy aircraft, the pilot was in a position to shoot. As he followed his target he would have to make sure that the floating bead was directed at the cockpit of his opponent. When he pressed his gun button, there would be a good chance he would achieve a kill.

The Second World War saw the introduction into service of fighter aircraft which were almost twice as fast as the biplanes they superseded. New types like the Kittyhawk, Spitfire and the German Messerschmitt Bf. 109 were capable of top speeds of 350 miles an hour (560km/hr) which meant that during a fight there was precious little time to aim. The lumbering biplanes of the 1930s used a rudimentary ring and bead sight. Now pilots had the gyro gunsight as well.

Most pilots were poor shots, so to give them a better chance of at least hitting something, the machine guns on the Spitfire were harmonised to give a 'shotgun' bullet pattern at the best firing range. This became known as the area of lethal density and it gave a poor marksman a good chance of destroying his adversary.

Clive Caldwell was a natural marksman who could hit a target with uncanny accuracy, but even he was not immediately successful in air combat. By June 1941 he had flown 40 operational sorties in the Western Desert, but had only shot down one aircraft.

Clive said: 'For about the first 30 sorties I did quite a bit of shooting and I wasn't hitting anybody. They didn't seem to notice me and I began to feel a little neglected . . . I had been hit two or three times and wasn't enjoying being on the receiving end.'

The solution was simplicity itself, and it was suggested by the position of the sun.

It was late afternoon and Clive was piloting a Tomahawk back across the desert when he noticed the shadows cast by the other aircraft in his flight as they sped over the sand. Almost absent-mindedly, his finger found the gun button and he fired a quick burst, noticing how the tracer rounds fell in relation to his shadow.

> . . . I suddenly realised the significance of these shadows racing across the sand. When I tried to shoot the shadow I missed. I was over and way behind. This was an immediate demonstration by contact registration of self-correcting the method of learning deflection shooting.

Over the next few days he experimented with the amount of deflection required whatever the speed of the aircraft. Within a month a signal was sent to all fighter squadrons in the Middle East telling them to adopt Caldwell's shadow shooting technique.

Clive continually practised his shooting and always told other pilots to do the same. There was a story that he scorned the use of the gyro gunsight and used the ring and bead sight instead. Others said that he marked a black dot on the canopy of the aircraft and drew a bead on his target using that. Whatever he used his score grew as swiftly as his reputation.

Clive wrote a treatise on shadow shooting which became required reading for all novice fighter pilots:

> The fighter pilot with no idea of how to shoot, who couldn't knock a sick parrot off a perch with a pick handle so to speak is nothing more than a potential loss flying about the sky, and virtually an expensive but useless passenger in a squadron.
>
> In fact, he is worse than useless, in as much as he occupies a seat in a highly efficient and specialised instrument of war which he renders impotent by his very lack of special skill to apply to the purpose for which it was designed, namely destroying the enemy.
>
> The seat could be better filled by a man more fitted for a particular job. Though his actual flying skill may even prompt him even to criticise certain birds for their inability to fly blind, upside down or in bad weather though he may possess physical and moral courage of the highest order, the dash of a d'Artagnan and a ruggedness of spirit that admits of no defeat no matter what the circumstances, all this is wasted and the very utmost he can do is to offer a threat to the enemy that he is unable to fulfil.
>
> His squadron commander is visualising his prospective profit and loss account with respect to his future dealings with the enemy can only see a blank space against this pilot's name on the profit side.
>
> Where conditions of terrain and weather make it possible, pilots have the advantage of learning to shoot or

improve their shooting by the best and most practical method yet discovered, that of shooting at the moving shadow of another aircraft.

By constant and faithful practice on the shadows the pilot can build up a repertoire of shots that he knows, likes and has confidence in, much as does a billiard player, and which he makes by recognition, and not calculation.

If he could hit the shadow regularly from a certain position and angle, opening fire when it looks about the right size having become used to seeing it that way and knowing by the pattern of his bullets that this is a best range and also accustomed to the necessary movements of his stick to retain his deflection, then instead of shadow it was an actual aircraft, flying a few feet above the surface then obviously he would shoot it down.

Remember that you can count on five bursts of fire only. When these have been used so are your chances of knocking down an enemy aircraft, therefore it is obvious that it is of little use taking shots that you don't know how to make and have no confidence in. Steep turn shots are particularly hard; for instance as when the right deflection has been allowed, the aircraft you are shooting at is well out of sight under your nose and you are shooting by memory, hoping he is still where you think he is.

Shots from below and behind are easier for a number of reasons. Firstly your own aircraft, the gun platform, is steadier in the climb than in the dive. It is easier to see the enemy aircraft and its line of flight against the sky and clouds than against the ground or water when its disruptive upper side camouflage to some extent distracts your eyes. You are more likely also to be unobserved when below and the enemy aircraft is in plain view at all times, not tending to disappear under your nose. In addition, he is more vulnerable to damage from below—petrol tanks, auxiliary gears, lower parts of the pilot's body or legs, undercarriage etc. The fact that you make an attack does not necessarily mean that you must fire your guns.

If the enemy aircraft, having observed your approach, takes appropriate avoiding action, quite obviously the shot is being made more difficult. If the avoiding action is such as to make it too difficult, complete the attack as far as sound tactical flying dictates, but do not open fire, as the odds are heavily against you hitting and you waste a fifth of your ammunition with nothing accomplished. It may be necessary often to make several attacks before being satisfied with the shot and opening fire. The only time when this does not apply is when you are scare shooting at any enemy in the hope of distracting him or driving him off the tail of one of your own machines. Therefore the thing is practise your shadow shooting as faithfully and as often as possible. Increase your repertoire of recognition shots. Fly for your shooting. Don't fire unless you really think you can hit. Hoping won't help you.

On 26 June 1941 Clive was once again escorting the Blenheim bombers to Gazala when they were pounced on by 30 Messerschmitt Bf. 109s.

Willy Messerschmitt's snub-nosed fighter was superior to

the Tomahawk in every way. It was faster, it climbed better, and it was more manoeuverable. When the Messerschmitt first appeared in the skies over Britain it had achieved a myth of invincibility, largely because it had only flown against inferior Polish and French aircraft. The Me-109 could go higher than the Tomahawk, Kittyhawk and Spitfire. But this was a battle fought low down at altitudes of between 5–10 000 feet. This is where the P 40 came into its own. As Clive wrote:

> While inferior in performance, particularly at altitude to the Messerschmitt Bf. 109 and to the elegant Macchi MC 202 Folgore which latter aircraft appeared in the desert towards the end of 1941 and excited my admiration if not my approval, the Tomahawk seemed to hang onto them well in a steep or vertical dive and operating within its own altitude limitations performed credibly in a dogfight.
>
> The Tomahawk's lack of comparable performance left the initiative mainly with the opposition and it was usual to accept their initial attack in order to engage at our best height. We rarely caught them below us.

On 26 June Clive was in luck; the Messerschmitt was below him.

He rolled the heavy American fighter on its back and went downhill like a roller coaster. He recalled the advice given by his boxing coach:

> Be light on your feet. Attack and retreat. The jab is a sharpshooter's key weapon. The very same components that

make the military sharpshooter an ominous foe also make the boxing sharpshooter a force to be reckoned with.

The Me-109 had no idea Clive was there. He slid in below and behind. At point blank range he opened fire in short bursts. The Me-109's splendidly engineered fuel injected engine was not enough to save it from taking a round through a coolant pipe. There was a spattering of oil on the front windscreen, and a sound like that of a child banging a biscuit tin with a stick. A piece of aluminium flew past Clive's ear. 'It was virtually a no deflection shot and I knew if I didn't hit this one I wasn't going to hit anything.'

The pilot, who was nineteen and lived with his mother in a small house in Regensburg, just had time to piss his pants before he died. It is possible he also caught a fleeting glimpse of the man in the Tomahawk who had killed him—a man with a pencil moustache undoing his oxygen mask. Then the desert rushed up and it was all over for him.

> I was totally bemused and delighted by this success. At last it CAN be done and I remember being most elated; so much so that I almost got myself shot down! I was so keen on watching this fellow go down and I should have been skidding away but I stayed after him and the next thing—bang!

Clive had been attacked from behind by another Messerschmitt.

> That took me away quick enough and fortunately the bloke behind me couldn't shoot much better than me. But I'd

made a start now although I realised that this fellow had been a bit of a 'gimmee'.

That night Clive thought of home and wrote about what he had done that day. After his first kill he decided to write his wife's name, Jean, on the gunsight of his aeroplane.

> It was bitter cold in the desert, and I thought of the fire in the lounge and the dogs dozing in front of it. I was hungry and miserable and I knew from looking at other fellows that I was dirty, muddy, and unshaven. We shivered for a while before we dropped off into an uneasy doze.

Eight thousand miles away Jean was sitting by that same fire thinking of her man. The couple had been living in a flat in Sydney but when Clive went to Egypt she had packed her things and gone back to Illabo.

They had spent little time together before Clive went off to war, and these were lonely times for Jean. Communications with the Middle East were virtually non-existent, and it took six weeks for a letter to reach him. It would be a long time before she would see him again. The dogs dozed and twitched in their sleep and a log fell into the hearth. Jean Caldwell put down her book. Clive Caldwell blew out the kerosene lamp in his tent and thought about tomorrow. If there was a tomorrow.

Not everybody from the squadron had come back that day.

They went into it like a child seeking adventure—like a small boy playing soldiers—without realising the implications of the game. They don't realise that high adventure will probably cost them their lives.

The Allies depended upon their supplies from the port of Tobruk which changed hands several times during the war in the desert. Caldwell and his squadron often found themselves protecting convoys from air attack. On 30 June, four days after Clive's first success he was in one of nine Tomahawks that were engaged by 20 Junkers 87 Stukas accompanied by 30 Me-109s and twin engined Messerschmitt 110s. The squadron shot down six aircraft without loss. Clive shot down two Stukas and shared in the destruction of a Me-110.

One of the Stukas was carrying Karl Rohde, a cine-cameraman hoping to record the action for the German newsreel company Deutsches Wochenschau.

The footage got left on the cutting room floor.

Clive did not fly exclusively against the Germans, and occasionally encountered mixed formations of the Luftwaffe and the Regia Aeronautica. The Italian fighters were slow and underpowered, although when flown by experienced pilots they could give a good account of themselves. In Libya at the outbreak of the war in the desert the Italians had a much larger air force than the RAF. The Fourth Stormo was considered a crack unit, and some of its pilots like Tenente Colonello (Wing Commander) Ernesto Botto had already become aces in the Spanish Civil War.

Early on in the desert war, the Italians flew an excellent biplane fighter, the Fiat CR 42 Falco (Falcon) which was faster than the Gloster Gladiator and more agile than the Hawker

Hurricane. This was succeeded by the Fiat G 50 Freccia (Arrow) the first Italian all-metal cantilever monoplane and a highly manoeuverable aircraft.

On 7 July 1941 the Tomahawks of 250 Squadron made a fighter sweep over Bardia. Clive got separated from the rest of the formation and late in the afternoon met two of the little Fiats. The two Fiats split up and dived left and right. Clive singled out the one on the right for attention. The Fiat was an odd looking machine with a hump in its nose. Originally the aeroplane had been fitted with a canopy, but this was disliked so much by its pilots that it had been abandoned, and the pilot was now protected from the slipstream by two sliding perspex screens which came up above his head.

God it must be cold in there, thought Clive, taking in the white cross on the rudder and the prancing black stallion on the fuselage. Then the incendiary rounds ripped into the fuselage and the aircraft dived into the ground. Clive had a friend who owned a Fiat car and it was always breaking down.

'FIAT', said Clive. 'What's that stand for? Fix It Again Tony? This G 50 dived and I was able to get in a further short burst. It crashed approximately one mile south of the road, but did not explode.'

Clive put the Tomahawk on the deck and set a course for home but his day was not yet over. He came across five camps of German motor transport each with about 40 vehicles, mostly armoured cars and light tanks. 'I ground strafed vehicles and personnel injuring and killing about a dozen of the latter and saw my bullets hit several vehicles.'

Later he wrote: 'I have no objection to hobnobbing with

the Germans, Japanese or Italians. But I wouldn't normally cross the street to meet one of them.'

The Italian pilots on average were considered to be better at aerobatics than the Germans or the British, but lacking in tactics when it came to air fighting. 'They were certainly very fine aerobatic pilots but seemed to enter combat more in the spirit of medieval joust than of a life and death struggle,' said Neville Duke.

Bobby Gibbes remembers engaging a Fiat CR 42 which proceeded to perform the most exquisite aerobatic display. 'I watched in admiration and then when he had finished I shot him down,' he said.

Rudolf Sinner of the Luftwaffe's II/JG 27 thought the Italians fine pilots not lacking in courage but always hampered by their equipment:

> We watched with compassionate admiration the gallant Macchi MC 202 pilots die in their flying crates besides the Stukas they had to protect.
>
> In combat they had nothing to offer, even after being equipped with excellent aircraft like the Macchi MC 202.

Later in the war the Italians would receive fighters like the Macchi Veltro (Greyhound) and the Folgore (Lightning) both powered by licence-built versions of the German Daimler-Benz engines. Caldwell admired the Greyhound enormously and thought it could have met the Allies on more equal terms if it had appeared earlier.

•

On the afternoon of 29 August 1941, while the sun made a spectacular descent into the Mediterranean, Caldwell had been airborne for an hour providing fighter cover for Allied shipping in the Gulf of Sollum but there was no sign of the enemy.

Clive was performing a routine which he personally found to be ineffectual and irritating—weaving. This is was the technique where two aircraft weaved backwards and forwards behind the squadron covering their tails from a surprise interception.

Clive's fellow weaver was an inexperienced Rhodesian pilot. The technique was that Clive would make a click with his radio transmitting button which was the signal to turn back the other way. But on this occasion he did not hear Clive's signal, and was 600 yards away and heading east.

By now Clive was angry and distracted. It was too late in the day to be wet nursing novice Rhodesian pilots, and there was hopefully a cold beer awaiting him back at base. He was concentrating on his wayward companion and could not have seen what was about to happen.

Lieutenant Werner Schroer of Jagdgeschwader 1/27 was flying a Messerschmitt Bf. 109, and Clive presented a splendid target. Schroer decided to use the machine guns first and aim for the centre of the aeroplane. Then the cannon, slower firing but very destructive.

The first cannon shell hit the side window and clattered on through the instrument panel. There was a tremendous bang and the Tomahawk's cockpit filled with smoke. Clive was astonished to see that part of the instrument panel had disappeared. There was a big chunk out of the wing and the trailing edges had opened up. It was like a silent movie. With his ears enclosed by headphones Clive could not hear the German aircraft firing but he could hear and feel the bullets hitting the Tomahawk.

You could feel the aircraft shaking and then more of these bloody bangs and noise.

I'm in a bad case. I'm hit through my left shoulder it was as though someone had hit me with a seven pound hammer and driven a six inch nail into me. That's what it felt like. Then I was hit in the back and in the neck and in the left leg which threw my foot off the rudders and up into the corner of the cockpit.

Another bullet hit my right earphone and twisted my helmet goggles and oxygen mask around over my face temporarily blinding me.

Instinctively, Clive pulled the stick back and brought his right foot hard down onto the rudder. The aircraft stalled and started spinning, and Clive blacked out. He had lost 500 feet before he came to and brought the aircraft under control.

Werner Schroer circled around, satisfied that he had shot Caldwell down. He returned to base and claimed him as a victory.

Now that he had time to think, the seriousness of Clive's situation overwhelmed him. 'I'm pretty upset. I'm obviously wounded.'

Fragments of perspex from the broken canopy had lodged

in his face, and the air coming through the holes in the side window had sprayed a fine mist of blood around the canopy.

This all made it look worse than it was, thought Clive with more than a touch of diffidence. His leg hurt, and when he put his hand down to his groin, it came back covered in blood. 'Oh Christ, there goes my manhood.'

To add to his troubles he had a small fire down on the right side of the cockpit which was producing oily smoke. The 12 cylinder Allison engine was running, according to Clive, in spits and farts, sometimes firing on ten cylinders sometimes fewer.

Clive was well out to sea and the aircraft appeared to be in its death throes. Unlike the English Channel, there were no air-sea rescue vessels if he came down in the drink. There was only one option: Clive had to get out. He pulled the canopy back and and tore off his helmet, the radio/telephone cable and the oxygen tube. If they were still attached they could break his neck when he left the aircraft. Then he pulled the pin from his safety harness and prepared to climb out.

But with the canopy open air rushed into the cockpit and the fire suddenly went out. Later Clive found it had been an oil fire caused by an incendiary round hitting the oil return pipe. He decided to stay with the aircraft and try to get home.

Clive was only 500 feet off the ground and when he crossed the coast near Sidi Barrani he saw a number of planes milling around in a manner suggesting an engagement.

As my plane seemed to answer the controls fairly well apart from turns I made a gradual turn and climbed back towards the said aircraft finally making an attack on what I believed to be Me-109F (this because it did not have standard Me-109 tailstruts).

Clive fought like a bull who had been goaded by picadors. He threw the Tomahawk about the sky, rivets popping from the aluminium skin like cherry stones. He did not know how seriously the aircraft had been damaged, and fully expected it to fall apart at any moment.

He might have had it, but he was damned if he wasn't going to take a Messerschmitt with him. The two German pilots were astonished at the ferocity of his repeated attacks; then one of them made the fatal error of overshooting him. Clive manoeuvered the Tomahawk into the best firing position and shot the Messerschmitt down into the sea.

So in a crippled aircraft and losing blood he had accounted for another German fighter!

Having previously lost the pin on my harness, I was holding the straps in my left hand for security which, together with the damage sustained to the aircraft made it inadvisable to attempt much in the way of a quick change of altitude, so I carried on straight to a very low level and continued to base, arriving 2010 hours without further incident.

When Clive got back to to Sidi Haneish, and painfully fumbled for the lever which raised and lowered the flaps, he flipped the lever but nothing happened—the flaps didn't work, so his landing run was longer than usual. 'I wasn't particularly badly hurt, and climbed out of the cockpit with the aid of my rigger, armourer and fitter.'

When the ground crew made a close examination of Clive's Tomahawk they found it had taken 108 machine gun rounds, and five cannon shells. It was the cannon shells that had wrecked the flaps and punctured a tyre.

Clive now faced a long and painful session on the makeshift operating table. Using long probes and tweezers two doctors, including one from the Royal Naval Fighter Squadron of the Fleet Air Arm, took about four and a half hours to remove all the fragments of shrapnel and perspex from Clive's shoulder, face, neck and leg. The leg wound was superficial, and Clive was relieved to find his manhood was not in any way threatened!

There was no anaesthetic apart from half a bottle of overproof rum, which Clive reported was 'taken internally'.

Later Clive wrote: 'Drink is no good to fly on. Drinking rum—a procedure calculated to result in a primary state of high optimism. As the author can testify.'

Only later in his tent did he reflect on the day:

I made a mistake then I was afraid; so terrified that my tongue clove to the roof of my mouth and I could hear my heart beating like a bass drum. I only had one wish: to escape the horror of the incineration and death that seemed inevitable inside the next few minutes or less. I was panting, dripping sweat and very tired.

I ask myself will life ever give me such joy again? I felt, with every nerve strung taut, doubly alive. It is all before me at this moment, the cold winter evening, the frosty white sky.

With his body a mass of small cuts sewn together with prickly sutures Clive found it difficult to sleep that night. Less than 43 miles away in the improvised officers' mess of the Luftwaffe's JG (Fighter Squadron) 27, Lieutenant Werner Schroer was being being toasted in schnapps by his fellow officers on the occasion of his sixth kill.

He had seen his bullets hitting Clive's Tomahawk and the aircraft going into a spin. But as he drained his glass he reflected uneasily that he had not actually seen Clive's aircraft hit the ground. Surely the Australian could not have survived?

Werner Schroer went on to claim 114 aircraft shot down— four times as many as Clive—including 61 in North Africa. He survived the war and died in Munich in 1985.

How many other German pilots, wondered Clive, had made exaggerated claims? The Allied pilots had limited operational "tours" and then were rested whereas the German pilots flew continuous operational missions; hence they racked up enormous scores; but their lists of victories were always open to question.

Clive enjoyed the war in the Western Desert. He responded warmly to the land, full of vibrant colours merging with the contrasting Mediterranean shoreline. The desert was a proper place to fight, Clive felt, with not much else to consider except the enemy. The fighting men could concentrate on their work for six to eight weeks at a stretch, then receive a few days' leave.

To be granted 48 hours clear leave meant a hurried search for the least filthy clothing, then hitching a plane ride to Cairo.

Shepheard's Hotel was the biggest in Cairo and the usual choice of venue. An airman on leave craved what was denied him in the desert—an unlimited supply of hot and cold water, plenty of fresh and tasty food, mixed company and comfort.

Pilots treated themselves to the luxury of a long soak in the bath followed by a visit to a barber. Although feeling thoroughly clean after bathing, the pilots would find that the barber could usually extract more dirt from his face and hair. There would be a wash, haircut and shave, and sometimes the removal of a beard. A face massage would completely remove the last traces of oil and grime.

Food and drink were expensive, but eagerly sought. Fruit and vegetables—virtually non existent in the desert—were most appreciated. Stella beer was drunk in huge quantities, and the locally brewed spirits were best avoided.

A *gari* would take the airman to a cabaret. The floor show would usually be performances of national dances, acrobats and singers. Girls of various nationalities—Egyptian, Russian, Greek—would be available as dancing partners for the exorbitant price of 4 shillings, which ostensibly bought the girl a drink. It looked like champagne but usually turned out to be ginger ale. Chaperones lined the walls.

Cairo shut down at midnight, and the pilots would retire to the day's final luxury—a soft bed and clean white sheets.

The next day's sightseeing was always preceded by breakfast in bed. When they hit the streets the airmen would be pestered by *Dragomen* selling everything from opium to cheap brass ornaments. If the pilots learned any Arabic at all it was the word *imshi* (piss off).

In the bazaars, shopkeepers would hawk their goods; there were snake charmers and trained monkeys, sellers of papyrus, small figurines of Tutankhamun or Anubis or Horus, shirts made of Egyptian cotton and carpets—always carpets. Clive journeyed out to the Pyramids and mused about the damage done to the face of the Sphinx by Napoleon's cannon balls.

In an idle moment Clive visited a Hindu palm reader. He told him of the aeroplanes he had shot down.

'Is that all you are worried about?' said the old man. 'Keeping score?'

'That has nothing to do with it at all,' said Clive brusquely.

'Well then,' said the fortune teller, 'Just keep on scoring.'

Clive was shocked. That night he wrote:

No compassion you see. Islam is going to turn this world upside down before this century is out. The Middle East will need keeping an eye on.

In Australia, it was some weeks before Jean heard by letter that Clive had been wounded. There were no phone calls and she had to rely upon the occasional radio reports or what she read in the newspapers, all of which was heavily censored. 'We were at the end of the world and the news was very slow coming over.'

Three days after being wounded Clive was back in the air, a bit sore and a bit more wary. Once again he was bounced by a Messerschmitt but this time he had the presence of mind to decline combat.

For the next seven weeks there was a lull in air fighting,

and Clive's flight switched its attention to escort duties and ground strafing. Clive thought that this was more important work than fighter sweeps over the desert looking for an air battle that may not eventuate. Often pilots went on patrol and saw nothing.

This he considered to be fighting for fighting's sake, just for the fun of it, so to speak. Clive also believed that if you were going to lose an aircraft it should be doing something worthwhile such as destroying enemy troops, supply dumps or aircraft on the ground—not just aimlessly looking for a fight in the air.

The desert had no cover; there were no forests that could hide tanks and soldiers. Caught in the open, men and machines were extremely vulnerable to attack from above. Clive believed that his pilots should take the battle to the enemy, ranging far and wide looking for targets of opportunity:

> For a year now I have lived with killings and can reasonably claim to have killed over 1000 men in the air or on the ground. If that meant disrupting enemy forces for a week or a few days it was worth it.

Things started to hot up again at the end of November 1941 with the start of Operation Crusader. On the ground British tanks had advanced through Cyrenaica, the eastern province of Libya aiming to engage and destroy General Erwin Rommel's Panzergruppe Afrika. In fact they found themselves pinned down by the artillery fire of Rommel's 90th Light Division.

On 23 November, a day on which British armoured

columns on the ground were forced to retreat, there was furious activity in the air with both sides claiming kills.

Clive had by now been promoted to Flight Lieutenant.

His flight met twelve Me-109s, six Junkers 87 twin-engined bombers and twelve Italian Fiat G 50s. The battle lasted twelve minutes, during which Clive shot down another Me-109E, and three of his sergeant pilots destroyed three more.

The main Allied bomber used in the desert was the twin-engined Bristol Blenheim which, by 1941, was coming to the end of its useful life. The Blenheims could never venture far without fighters to protect them.

At 3.30 that November afternoon, nine Blenheims took off to give support to South African troops on the ground who were advancing on the Sidi Rezegh area. Five Tomahawks were provided as top cover by 250 Squadron. All the way there the formation was attacked by Me-109s and Clive managed to shoot down another.

Whether he liked it or not Clive was acquiring celebrity status, although some found him far from unassuming. Roderick Owen, a British writer said:

Killer Caldwell survived the desert battles. Unlike either 'Imshi' Mason, a British pilot from Blackpool, or the German ace Hans Joachim Marseille, he was a cool machine for destruction with no doubts as to his own efficiency, with little of the usual modesty as to his achievements. A lone wolf, he was at his best when there were experiments to be carried out—for instance he dropped the first bomb from a Kittyhawk.

'Imshi' Mason and Marseille were at their most deadly when working with a group (their tactics, curiously similar, depended upon shadowing and pouncing); Caldwell, the one against the world, seemed almost to be a heroic survivor from another era in the swashbuckling Elizabethan tradition.

But although there was still room for the individual hero, the Middle East air aspect was changing. Aircraft were rarely to be employed in ones and twos, more often in fours and eights. Soon, whole wings and even whole groups would be in the air at once, as the increase in resources made this practicable.

The Stuka party

The Junkers 87 Stuka was a bully boy of a machine; a vile predatory thing not so much an aeroplane as a propaganda weapon. Fitted to the wing was a siren driven by the wind, designed to terrify helpless civilians.

The sight of this vulture sitting squarely in the cross-hairs was the dream of every fighter pilot. There were no laser guided bombs in 1941, but the Stuka could place a bomb within 330 feet of the target. Ugly it was, but it was flown by the most highly decorated Knights Cross winner of the war, Hans Ulrich-Rudel, who claimed to have destroyed more than 500 Allied tanks. It was not just a bomber; the twin Mauser machine guns which poked out of the radio operator's window should always be treated with respect.

Clive Caldwell had no less than 40 Stukas in his sights on 5 December 1941 when his formation engaged a mixed German and Italian force three times its size. There were twelve Tomahawks from 250 Squadron and ten from 112 Squadron. Clive led the attack on the Stukas and 112 went for the fighters, a mixture of German Me-109s and Italian Fiat G 50s.

> I received radio warning that a large enemy formation was approaching from the north-west. No 250 squadron went into line astern behind me and as No 112 squadron attacked the escorting enemy fighters we attacked the JUs from the rear quarter. At 300 yards I opened fire with all my guns at the leader of one of the rear section of three, allowing too little deflection and hit number two and number three, one of which burst into flames immediately and the other going down smoking. I then attacked the leader of the rear section from below and behind opening fire with all guns at very close range. The enemy aircraft turned over and dived steeply . . . I was able to pull up the belly of the one at the rear holding the burst until very close range. The enemy aircraft diced gently straight ahead streaming smoke and then dived into the ground.

It was an astonishing feat of markmanship. Clive had shot down five aircraft in eighteen seconds, hitting two aircraft with one three-second burst of fire! To become a fighter ace you had to shoot down five aircraft.

Clive had become an instant ace! But it might have been a different story if Clive had tackled the fighters.

'It should be noted that, although not to be underestimated, Stukas were relatively easy, really,' said Clive modestly.

This battle was fought at low level, and the Australian troops below had a grandstand view of the action. There were many witnesses to Clive's kills. 'Because of this,' said Clive, 'confirmation was easier than usual.'

Later in his diary he wrote:

> To kill a man is no worry. At first you think about it a little but you soon get over that. It's your life or theirs. This is war. You do what you have to do then forget it. All rules of civilian life are suspended and you find yourself doing and thinking all manner of things that you never thought you could do.

'The kite was no good to me so I took to the brolly.' The speaker was Bobby Gibbes of 3 Squadron Royal Australian Air Force, who described how he bailed out of a crippled aircraft. *Taking to the brolly* is a euphemistic description for a stressful situation when a pilot has to vacate the cockpit because the aeroplane is not working very well. Most pilots do not wish to be parachutists, and see no sense in leaving a perfectly good aeroplane.

This is easier said than done. For a start, the aeroplane has to slow down to a speed which makes it possible to get over the side of the cockpit and throw yourself into the slipstream. At speeds of 300 miles an hour, a pilot is pinioned into his seat and it almost impossible to do this. The secret is to set the elevator trim wheel so that the aircraft flies nose up, open the cockpit and turn the aircraft on its back and fall out. But then there is still the chance that you will strike the tail.

During the war pilots were given this advice: 'When a prang (crash) seems inevitable endeavour to strike the softest, cheapest object in the vicinity as slowly and gently as possible.'

Unlike Gibbes, Clive never had to take to the brolly. He did however have some lucky escapes.

Once, he was doing an early morning strafing run on a German aerodrome when he was hit by ground fire. 'I had a big hole in the starboard wing of the aeroplane, but when I put the undercarriage down it seemed to be alright.'

But the wheels had not lowered, and before he knew it, the Kittyhawk was tumbling along the runway like a Catherine wheel, scattering pieces of metal in all directions. The machine came to rest in a cloud of dust. Clive was upside down in the cockpit still strapped in his seat with his head just centimetres from the ground.

There was a strong smell of 100 octane petrol and Clive noticed that the ignition switches were still on. Fuel was pouring from the aircraft, and it would take only the smallest spark to ignite it. The textbook approach was turn all the switches off to avoid a fire. But Clive decided not to in case any of the electrical wires had broken loose in the crash.

The big thing is you go through the formality of switching off. I thought I wouldn't just in case all the these switches weren't fully connected and maybe we got a little spark.

The accident had been witnessed by many on the ground, but the first to reach the smashed aircraft as it ground to a stop was a young British anti-aircraft gunner who manned one of the ack-ack positions guarding the airfield. He was armed with a spade or, as Clive described it, an entrenching tool.

> I have been involved in a number of crashes, many of them my own fault, but I was concerned because of the exuberance of a very friendly ack-ack gunner who immediately charged to my rescue. I was very alarmed because of the determined look on his face; he was obviously going to dig, and I had the canopy back fortunately.

Clive was unbuckling his harness when the gunner charged at him with the spade. He was intending to dig into the soil around the cockpit so that Clive could crawl out.

The dry shale had been so hardened by the desert sun that it was like digging into rock. On the gunner's first thrust, the spade glanced off the shale, and hit the canopy with a resounding smack, dangerously close to Clive's face.

Clive had survived the accident and did not now wish to suffer immolation. The gunner was not much more than eighteen years old. Clive addressed him very firmly giving him recommendations and advice in the colourful language of a Sydney taxi driver.

'What the fucking hell do you thing you are doing?' he shouted. 'Can't you smell petrol? You'll blow us both to smithereens.'

Clive's blistering tirade lasted for nearly a minute. The young gunner stood with his mouth open.

'I was trying to save your life, Sir,' he said sheepishly.

After Clive had calmed down he told the gunner to get some help to lift up the tail so that he could get out. 'I urged him to get a body of strong men and walk the tail up for me which he did and I scrambled out.'

The seriousness of his escape overwhelmed him, and Clive suddenly felt a great tiredness. His head spun and his throat was dry, and he sat down heavily on the ground. He was resting his head on the shale when a pair of army boots hove into his field of vision. They belonged to the sergeant in charge of the gun battery.

The sergeant spoke in a North Country accent: 'I didn't like the way you spoke to the lad, Sir.'

Clive replied, 'Sergeant, I was a little overwrought, you must forgive me.'

He said, 'Well, we don't normally use language like that, Sir.'

The aeroplane was a total write-off, but Clive somehow had survived.

Clive's score was rising rapidly. After the Stuka party, his aircraft had fourteen black Balkankreuz crosses painted under the cockpit and two circular white discs bearing three axes strengthened by a bundle of sticks (the markings of the Italian fascists). On Boxing Day 1941, Clive belatedly received a bar to his Distinguished Flying Cross. His score was to rise to eighteen by the New Year. But further decorations were not immediately forthcoming.

The commanding officer of 238 Wing told Clive that he

had recommended him for a DSO and gave him a copy of the citation. He never received it at the time and learned at the end of the war that it had been denied him because:

> This officer is an Empire Air Trainee and as such is considered to be already sufficiently decorated and is to receive no more regardless of further service.

The letter was signed by the Chief of the Air Staff, George Jones. Obviously, the career officers back in Australia still had little regard for the Empire Air Trainees.

On the ground, Rommel had now begun a fresh offensive in an attempt to drive the Eighth Army into Egypt. Once again the RAF squadrons switched to ground strafing the Afrika Corps. On one day 250 Squadron flew no less than 69 separate sorties, a record for a fighter squadron.

Six days into the new year Clive was promoted to the rank of squadron leader and given command of the RAF's 112 Squadron, which was now re-equipping with the new Kittyhawk 1As. Clive had risen from pilot officer to squadron leader in twelve months—a record for promotion in the RAAF. He also became the first Empire Air Training scheme graduate to command a fighter squadron.

Caldwell became Neville Duke's commanding officer:

> He was a super Commanding Officer and he came to us just at the right time. Morale was sagging a bit at that time we were losing a lot of people—109s.

After the Crusader operation, losses were pretty heavy and he raised the squadron back up again.

He was a terrific character.

Duke and many of the other pilots regarded Caldwell as a senior citizen, because they were only in their twenties and he was ten or eleven years older. They had already flown together in mixed formations, but this was the first time they had met.

He was an extremely natural marksman and a most aggressive fighter pilot.

He led from the front; he was always the first in; he wasn't so much a tactician as a chap who would dive in at the deep end and take on anything that was going. We had a great admiration for him.

Duke found Clive very hard to keep up with socially in the bar.

Not that we had much to drink anyway. We had the Cairo run which used to come up once a month with the beer which was rationed out.

The squadron became famous for its sharkmouth insignia. The pearly white teeth of the great white shark might have have offered a psychological advantage over superstitious Asians, but not the Germans. The truth was that the Messerschmitt in all its versions was a vastly superior aircraft to the Tomahawk and the Kittyhawk. The Luftwaffe could always dictate the terms of battle. They had the speed, the height and the firepower. The pilots, however, didn't always have the experience.

Which idiot let himself be shot down?

A pattering of rain on the red desert floor and a grumble of thunder. Near to the Australian tents a camel threw its head towards the sky and made a barking noise.

'Thank Christ,' said Caldwell. 'It was as hot as Marble Bar, now it's raining.'

Even in the desert sometimes it rains. Seeds dormant for years suddenly put out shoots. Flowers bloom. On that day, 21 February 1942, rain, low cloud and erratic sandstorms meant that you couldn't see a thing so the flight of six Messerschmitts did not get into the air until midday.

Lieutenant Hans-Arnold Stahlschmidt of 1/JG 27, a combat veteran with 59 victories, was uneasy about flying that day. He had reluctantly allowed himself to have his picture taken by some soldiers just before he took off. This was considered to be bad luck.

The engineers fitted a huge starting handle to the side of the engine and wound it up like a clockwork toy. He heard the whirring sound of the big flywheel then engaged the starter clutch control by pulling out the handle close to his left knee. There was a grinding noise then the propeller turned and the engine caught. Stahlschmidt swung the canopy closed, reflecting on how difficult it would be to get out if he crashed upside down.

He pushed the throttle forward and saw in the rear view mirror the ground crew disappearing in a cloud of dust. Of course Marseille was in the lead. Bloody Marseille. Nobody else got a look in with Marseille around.

The six Messerschmitts formed themselves into three rottes (pairs) and were climbing when they first saw the Kittyhawks of 112 Squadron. Stahlschmidt was flying the slowest aircraft of the six. Often identical types of aircraft were marginally faster or performed better than one another, and Stahlschmidt had drawn the lame duck.

He was so busy concentrating on the Kittyhawks that he did not notice his speed had dropped and he had fallen behind the others. Suddenly a plane with shark's teeth dragged itself up into a vertical climb, firing as it came, the aircraft seemingly hanging on the propeller. It was Caldwell.

Two other aces witnessed this fabulous shot. One was Hauptmann Gerhard Homuth, the other Hans Joachim Marseille. Homuth had shot down 46 aircraft, and Marseille 158.

Stahlschmidt's aircraft, meanwhile, caught fire and rolled

into a spin. Homuth hit the transmit button his radio and shouted, 'Which idiot let himself be shot down?'

At the last minute, Stahlschmidt managed to regain control of his Freidrich and made a crash landing in No Man's Land. It was his lucky day. He was picked up by a German patrol and was back at his base at Martuba that evening.

Caldwell's shot had been impressive, but the eleven Kittyhawks now found themselves at a serious disadvantage. Not only were they below the five remaining Messerschmitts, but they were about to be attacked by two of the most experienced pilots in the Luftwaffe. Two Polish fliers, Sergeant Derma and Flying Officer Jander were shot down, while Sergeant Elliott's Tomahawk was badly damaged and crashed near El Adem, the pilot later dying of his wounds.

Bobby Gibbes who flew with the RAAF's 3 Squadron had witnessed on another occasion Caldwell's technique of pulling the aircraft up vertically to attack aircraft flying overhead.

They came over going anti-clockwise way out of range. There were three of them in line astern going over us probably a thousand feet higher. We were probably 10–15 000 feet and they were 1000 feet above us. Caldwell, who was leading the wing that day, pulled up and had a squirt at it.

The thing went chunk chunk . . . He didn't shoot it down but he certainly hit it. It was a great shot.

I was just about to say, you bloody line shooting bastard Caldwell!

•

Neville Duke, a modest and charming man, sat on his lounge in Hampshire, and recalled Clive Caldwell and the war in the desert.

We were thrown together so much more in the desert than in the UK. You could spend three months in the desert before we got any leave in Cairo, so every night we were listening to Lili Marlene, gathered around the camp fire.

The pilots had their own words to Lili Marlene.

'Twenty thousand rounds of armour plated shell
You can press the tit my son and blow the Kraut to hell
Then you can press the tit old son
And blow the Kraut to Kingdom come
And poor Marlene's boyfriend
Won't see him any more.'

We used to wear all sorts of clothes—we weren't very uniform conscious—and was the occasion when the squadron was presented with the colours by Sir Arthur Coningham. There was Clive, dressed up in his uniform, looking terribly smart—first time I had ever seen him in a proper uniform.

We used to wear our badges of rank because we wanted to be identified as combatants. Some had khaki battle dress, some had blue tops, some flew in shorts and flying boots, and some designed their own uniforms around some barathea. Slightly unwashed as well—there wasn't much water to spare.

It was a bit primitive, in so much as the Australians

would go out into the bundu with a spade to do what they had to, otherwise the latrines were very matey with two or three thunderboxes together behind a bit of sacking. That was your privacy, so you got to know each pretty well.

The Australians received lots of food parcels from home, which the Brits never got, so we used to share that out around the tent. It was much more a private war. That type of air fighting—it was more reminiscent of World War I.

Most of the airfields were landing grounds cut out of the desert, or desert scrub was levelled off to make a landing area normally square airfields or square landing grounds.

El Adem was a more luxurious place. A proper airfield.

The Jerries moved out we moved in. Or the other way coming back we moved out they moved in. So it was always the same airfields like Gambut, Martuba, Gazala.

Sand was a major problem. You got sand on your canopy; it was attracted by the static so the sand remained on the canopy with the sun shining through the perspex—you couldn't see anything.

So if you were unfortunate on take-off you got somebody else's take-off blowing across you. Hopefully, the Germans had the same problem. On another operation when Clive was leading, I had the same problem on take-off so really I should have come back from that operation.

I was droning around Tobruk somewhere, and the next thing I knew the whole squadron was peeling off. I couldn't see what they were after, but I guessed there was something going to happen, so I followed them—and I didn't see the 109 that hammered me due to the sand and the perspex.

How did you come out of that?

Well, not very happily; he knocked bits off me and I lost half the elevators and one aileron and flaps and the holes in the wing, and I had to crash land at Tobruk. (Duke was flying a Tomahawk and a shell splinter damaged his leg.)

Did you find yourself flying with Caldwell very often—in the same formation?

Yes. We used to fly in fluid sixes or fluid fours. So you might be leading a section. He'd be leading a whole section of six or eight.

So if you were intercepted, what was the standard interception pattern?

If we were bounced from your six o'clock you'd turn into it—do a turn about—face the enemy. And then, of course, they pulled up so all you could do would be another turn about and watch for them to come down again. So round you'd go again.

Can you recall any other operations with Clive?

You had other people like Sailor Malan—he'd be leading the wing. So if there was a target or something he'd detach a section or a flight and he'd stay up there and organise the operation. But Clive was like the rest of us as soon as we saw anything. If you weren't leading then of course you'd report it and then the leader would say lead on and you'd go on after it but if Clive saw it he wouldn't detach you to go after it he'd be after it full bore, he'd pile in after it.

He'd just say something at twelve o'clock . . . down!

I can't see him in a peacetime air force. He was ideally suited to this loner type operation in a desert environment; it seemed natural to him.

When was it all over in North Africa?

In May 1943. I finished my tour and went back to the Canal Zone. Cairo. I was instructing on Spits and Kittyhawks. I was the CFI on Spitfires.

The last time you saw Clive?

April 1942.

The main thing was the boosting of morale. When he came to the squadron he was the right chap at the right time at the right place.

What do you remember most about him?

His ferocious ability at the bar. We regarded him as a father figure. And he was a good leader.

Clive was an established ace by the time John Waddy was posted to the desert. Like Clive, Waddy was a fellow Sydneysider, although he had very little combat experience.

Clive told him that if he survived his first three dog-fights he would probably live to become a fighter pilot. Clive took him on his first combat mission and told him: 'Stick to my tail like a leech.'

Waddy did as he was told and flew tight on Clive's tail. For the first time, he felt the jittery, excited feeling in his stomach as they chased all over the sky. Waddy was temporarily distracted when he saw puffs of smoke. The next minute he saw Clive in a climbing turn with Messerschmitts in hot pursuit.

Clive was doing things with his Tomahawk that Waddy (though sensibly not in Clive's ear) loudly cursed him for— they were upside down, on their backs, on their sides, all at 200 mph (320 km/ph).

Just as Waddy was thinking he'd be killed, he realised that he and Clive were flying inside a circle of planes that were going in the opposite direction. The enemy planes continued as a blur until Clive and Waddy suddenly found themselves alone in the sky. They waved to one another and headed for home.

I didn't have a clue that I'd had been in my first dog-fight until I landed. I felt awful that I hadn't fired a shot, just spent all my time following Clive's aircraft.

Clive was ice cool. 'Oh, it was a pretty good dog-fight up there while it lasted,' he said.

John Waddy must have learned something from Clive. He ended the war having shot down fifteen aircraft, and later went on to become a successful politician in the New South Wales parliament.

In other theatres of war officers and men had separate messes, but in the desert, Clive had decided that the mess would be for all aircrew. He had put the proposition to Air Marshal Tedder, who was interested in the psychology of supporting fighting men, that officers and men should mingle socially, and Tedder agreed.

Clive thought that demarcation through rank was absurd, especially as the Air Force was made up of young men from a wide range of civilian occupations; they were draftsmen and engineers, accountants and jackeroos, dentists and lawyers. He could not contemplate eating and relaxing apart from the other men.

He also believed that it was only over a few quiet beers in the mess that information and opinions could be properly shared, making for a stronger fighting group. Clive spoke earnestly, too, of drinking together as a good way of getting to know how people were responding to the mental strains of being a fighter pilot. He felt that he could make clearer judgments by observing the way people spoke informally about the day's events, by their tone and the words used, than by simply reading their formal reports.

It was in the mess that many new pilots received advice from Clive, even before engaging the enemy. He could tell them quite a bit over a quiet beer.

The Star of Africa

Caldwell often said he would not cross the street to meet a German but he might have made an exception in the case of Hans-Joachim Marseille, his opposite number in the Luftwaffe. They never shook hands but they met in the air more than once.

Caldwell was tall and shy, with a dislike of publicity. Marseille was short, blonde and extroverted. Caldwell was a man's man. Marseille was a serial womaniser and continually boasted about his affairs with movie stars. In Germany, girls papered their bedrooms with Marseille's photograph and he received sacks of fan mail even in the desert. Marseille had the profile of a rock star. Thanks to the propaganda machine manipulated by Dr. Joseph Goebbels, he became known in Germany as *The Star of Africa*. But at home he had constantly been in trouble for breaches of discipline.

One damaging comment in his service record reads

'Fliegerische Unzucht' which roughly translated means 'flying obscenity'. He was constantly being ticked off for low flying, steep climbing take-offs, and circling church steeples when weddings were taking place. Once he landed on one of Hitler's new autobahns just to prove that he could do it.

To Clive's irritation *he* had also become a pin-up in Australia. In Sydney, the Women's Auxiliary Combined Service Sub-Branch of Anzac House launched an appeal in the national newspapers exhorting people to buy a button for 'Killer'. The caption read:

An Outstanding Figure, An Air Killer of Enemy Flyers. In real life Wing Commander Clive Caldwell popularly known and admiringly referred to as 'Killer' Caldwell DSO DFC and Bar Polish Cross of Valour. Buy and wear a button for Killer.

Whether Clive liked it or not, the epithet had stuck.

But whereas Caldwell was a team leader, Marseille was a one-man band. In the air, Marseille's fellow pilots rarely had any chance to shoot down aircraft themselves. The boss did all the work. Their job was to beat off any attacking aircraft. This, more than anything, explains Marseille's extraordinary claim of 158 kills, all but four of which were in the desert.

In his new role as commanding officer of 112 Squadron, Clive was soon making waves with the top brass. For some time he had been critical of the role of escorting the slow Blenheim bombers. Fully laden with bombs the Blenheim could not fly much faster than 100 miles an hour, which meant that the Kittyhawks were at stalling speed and vulnerable to attack by German fighters. Clive lodged a formal protest to the AOC of the Desert Air Force, Air Vice Marshal Arthur 'Maori' Coningham and the Commander-in-Chief, Air Marshal Arthur Tedder. A direct result of this was the development of what became colloquially known as the Kitty-bomber.

The Blenheim could drop bombs but, it was not a fighter. The fighter-bomber version of Kittyhawk could do both. The P 40 was ideally suited to ground attack, and was a solid gun platform. How much more effective it could be, reasoned Clive, if it carried bombs as well. He discussed with the ground engineers the fitting of a 250-pound bomb on the centreline of the aircraft. His logbook records:

March 10 1942 in Kittyhawk AK-900. Test of type as fighter bomber. 250 lbs bomb hung centre. Angle of dive 45 degrees. Height 7000 feet—drop 3000 feet. Speed 300 miles an hour. No throw away gear. Bomb observed to miss the airscrew by a narrow margin.

The next day, 11 March, Clive tested the Kitty-bomber for the first time in action:

Took 250 lb bomb and dive bombed enemy fighter drome at Martuba. Bomb landed short of aircraft among tents etc. Strafed.

What Clive's logbook fails to record is that the dropping of the first bomb was preceded by a heavy drinking session which had started at lunchtime that day. The English pilot Neville Duke was one of the pilots at the party.

Duke had assumed there would no more flying that day, as the party had been going for five hours, and the sun was about to set. The group was fairly inebriated when one of the ground engineers arrived, gave Clive a smart salute and announced: 'Your aircraft is ready, Squadron Leader Caldwell.'

'Oh well,' said Clive, 'I'd better go and sling this bomb at something.

It was nearly dusk by the time he got into the air.
Duke recalled:

Suddenly Clive vanishes, takes off with this thing with a bomb on board. Flies over to Martuba which is the base from which the 109s are operating at that time and threw it in their direction. I don't know if it hit anything at that time. But it was was typical of Clive.

I don't say he had a lot to drink but he didn't seem to be affected by drink anyway, not on this occasion. But if you go on all night long drinking he'd he just be the same at the end as in the beginning.

The Kitty-bomber was an outstanding success and it was not long before most of the aircraft were fitted with bomb racks to carry 250- or even 500-pound bombs under the fuselage or under the wings. (Later the Kitty-bombers were to be used in the Pacific war.) Clive was to lead eight Kitty-bombers on the first attack against a German airfield at Derna. They did three times as much damage as a full squadron of Blenheims.

But there were disadvantages in turning the Kittyhawk into a fighter-bomber. Returning from bomb runs, the Kittyhawks were usually flying even lower than usual making them sitting ducks to the prowling Messerschmitts. The Germans do not record how many of their victories were against returning fighter bombers, but it would explain the high scores of Marseille, Schroer, Stahlschmidt and others.

Clive loved playing little games with those under his command. Like others in the squadron, Neville Duke occasionally let his hair down at boozy parties.

One morning back in March 1941 he was told to report to Caldwell.

When I marched into his office and saluted I thought he looked at me rather bleakly

'Anything on your mind, Duke?' he asked abruptly.

I thought hastily about one or two boisterous parties. It couldn't be anything to do with them.

'No, Sir.'

'Quite sure?'

Caldwell grinned and winked at him while he produced a DFC ribbon.

Groupy told me to give you this. It's an immediate award. Congratulations.

Duke had now been credited officially with eight enemy aircraft —two in England and six in the desert.

There was quite a session that night, and although I faded away at half past one in the morning, the party was still going strong.

America had been in the war since December 1941 and American fighter and bomber pilots were now beginning to appear in the desert. The big B 24 Liberator bombers had been in action against shipping and harbour facilities, and American P 40 Tomahawks were flying escort and strafing missions.

One night in the mess Clive met a young American pilot.

'You a pursoot pilot?'

(Americans called fighters pursuit aircraft.)

'Yes,' said Clive.

'You seen any action?'

'Oh yes, a bit,' said Clive.

'You'll see plenty before you've finished,' nodded the American, 'I've been on seven missions.'

'You have?' replied Caldwell.

'I sure have. How many have you been on?'

'Oh,' Clive paused to calculate and said in a quiet voice, 'About a hundred and eighty.'

The American's eyebrows shot up
'Say what do you live on buddy, birdseed?'

Clive Caldwell looked at the toy aeroplane with a wry smile. This was not a high powered fighter like the Kittyhawk, but a simple training aeroplane with an open cockpit. It had been delivered to the base at Gambut for the personal use of his commanding officer, Group Captain Cross. But now Clive was going to fly it.

The Miles Magister could be flown from either cockpit, but it was usual for the instructor to fly the aircraft from the rear seat. His passenger was the squadron doctor, a young man called Reg Solomon, fresh out of university. Solomon had never been in an aeroplane. Said Clive:

> He was wearing two rings on his uniform showing that he had absolutely no knowledge of medicine but he was with a fighter squadron and believed firmly that the whole object of being there required him to be in the air.

Group Captain Cross had been looking forward to flying the Magister with all the excitement of a child waiting for a Christmas present. He even telephoned Clive to ask what colour it was.

'I have no idea,' said Clive quite honestly for he had not yet seen the aircraft.

Flying an unarmed trainer aircraft in a war zone could present problems. As the airfield was constantly under attack by the Germans, the commanding officer suggested that two of the squadron's Kittyhawks maintain a patrol above.

'Take it easy,' said the CO. 'You've got no radio. We might get a raid on a couple of snappers come in and knock you down.'

Clive thought, 'How could I possibly come to harm in that tuppenny-halfpenny little thing?'

The take off from the rough desert strip was uneventful, and the little Magister was airborne in 300 yards. Pilot and passenger were sitting uncomfortably high on their parachute packs and dinghies. Clive leaned forward and gave the doctor a tap on the back to let him know that he was about to perform a few gentle aerobatics.

I did little gentle stall turn and I thought he might like a little negative G, so I pulled the stick up and gave it a push forward—and all the noise immediately stopped.

The doctor seemed quite unconcerned that the engine had stopped and still seemed to be enjoying the ride. Clive, meanwhile, was attempting to restart the engine, and looking for a beach to land on. He pumped the throttle and threw the aeroplane from side to side, but still the engine refused to start. By now the Magister was getting perilously low, and the only course of action seemed to be a forced landing. But where? Clive started looking for a place to land.

Gambut aerodrome was on an escarpment, but the ground below it was studded with large rocks. When the Magister was 500 feet above the ground, Clive made one last attempt to start the engine. It failed.

'It was now quite obvious what was going to happen,' said Clive.

Clive tapped his passenger on the shoulder again and told him to hang onto the crash pad in front because it wasn't going to be so good. But instead he grabbed onto the bottom of the seat.

> I thought the best thing to do was to write the undercarriage off before we start to look like strawberry jam ourselves. We hit one large rock, we sideslipped into it then we lost the wings, then the engine went, then the tail and just the bare fuselage and these twisted engine bolts.

When the aircraft finally came to rest Solomon was quite still and Clive thought he had broken his neck.

> So I got out and touched him on the cheek and he woke up and I said 'This is as far as we go.' He said, 'I don't think very much of that.' I said, 'I thought I did a pretty good job.' He said, 'I don't think so at all.'
>
> I said 'you clot'. The engine had stopped. I thought I did a wonderful job.
>
> He said, 'I thought you were going to do a trick?' I said, 'For Christ's sake, what more do you want?'

The two aviators staggered back from the wrecked aeroplane, and were taken back to their unit in a car driven by Bobby Gibbes of 3 Squadron RAAF.

'You're lucky,' said Clive when they arrived back at the

squadron. 'These pilots haven't had half the fun you've had in the last 20 minutes.'

The doctor asked, 'Have you ever seen an appendectomy?'

'No,' said Clive.

'Well it's no good criticising me for not knowing what goes on in an aeroplane. You're supposed to be a good pilot. I didn't know you were going to bugger it up to that extent!'

•

Of the 1300 Allied aircraft which the Germans claimed to have shot down in the desert, half of them were claimed by only fifteen pilots.

Most of the German pilots who came to the desert were much more experienced than the British, Australian and South African pilots. Allied pilots did tours and when they got war-weary they were moved out of the operational areas for rest and recuperation. Most of the German pilots however stayed in the desert until the final retreat.

This meant that the Allies were often fielding pilots with little or no operational experience at all. Caldwell subscribed to the German view of a unit comprising highly experienced pilots—a squadron of professional hunters.

Like Caldwell, Neville Duke's combat kills had all been from flying Tomahawks and Kittyhawks. Now they were to be replaced with Spitfires—an aircraft which was much more closely matched with the Messerschmitt. Clive envisaged a crack Spitfire unit, Neville Duke recalled:

He had the notion that he would form a squadron of experienced fighter pilots. We had the system that you did a tour of 200 hours then you went off on a rest.

So we had a lot of pilots with a modest amount of experience for a second tour, whereas the Germans had a lot of very experienced pilots all the time increasing their experience so Clive's idea was to have something like that.

But it didn't get anywhere because some people thought that was a bit elitist. It didn't go down too well with the powers that be. It never happened.

In fact it did nearly happen. Caldwell's idea sat well with Arthur Tedder. He told Caldwell that he was to be given command of a new Spitfire wing with three squadrons—two from Britain and the third to be made up of experienced desert fighter pilots. But for the intervention of the German navy, Clive would have taken command of his squadron. A freighter carrying Spitfires was torpedoed by a U-boat, others were sent for the defence of Malta and only one squadron was assigned to the Middle East.

Caldwell's idea finally germinated the following year. In March 1943 a special flight of highly experienced Polish pilots under Squadron Leader Skalski was formed inside 145 Squadron RAF. During their short stay in North Africa, the Poles accounted for 25 enemy aircraft.

Clive had flown with a number of Polish pilots and had won their admiration. Now he was to receive one of the highest Polish honours, the Croix des Vaillants.

The citation read:

Granted in appreciation of his buoyant co-operation with
Polish pilots when commanding Fighter Squadron Middle
East.

It was the first award of its kind to be made by the Poles
to a member of the Dominion Air Force.

On leave in Cairo in May 1942, Clive was drinking at the
Continental Hotel when he met the distinguished Australian
war correspondent, Kenneth Slessor, who wrote:

... met 'Killer' Caldwell, a tall, lanky, close-moustached
easy-smiling typical Australian, by no means averse to talking
about his exploits. He is now about to make a trip to England
and the USA and said he hoped to have a 'few games' in
England (i.e. go into action against Germans there).

Caldwell expounded a frank theory about 'gong hunting'
(i.e. collecting decorations). Admitted he was out to get all
he could, since these, and the publicity would be his only
assets after the war in getting a peacetime job. Must say I
agree with him.

Clive's final victories in the desert were on 14 March and 23
March 1942 when he destroyed a Macchi 202 fighter and
another Me-109.

On 19 February the Japanese had bombed Darwin and
Clive Caldwell was needed at home. Tedder's efforts to keep
Clive by proposing he lead a new Spitfire wing had failed.

Clive was reluctant to leave the field he knew was more exciting than the Pacific war could be, but had to go. The desert party was over.

Clive made his last flight in the Western Desert on 6 May 1942. It was a sunset patrol and there was no sign of the enemy. High in the sky it stayed light a little longer than on the ground and the Kittyhawk seemed to hang motionless in the air. All the aggression drained out of him and he suddenly felt a strange sense of peace. He thought of all the good men he had flown and fought with. Of Don Munro, a sergeant pilot from Moree whose charred body had been found in the wreck of his Tomahawk.

> This was his bounty for volunteer service in the field, and
> he would have judged it an acceptable one, I think.

Soon he would be seeing Jean again for the first time in nineteen months. She had been a faithful correspondent, and there had been a regular flow of letters, but it was a long time since he had heard the sound of her voice. How much should he tell her of what he had seen and done? How would she feel about the danger and the killing?

At school he had excelled at English and a line from *Othello* came to mind:

> She loved me for the dangers I had pass'd,
> And I loved her that she did pity them.
> This only is the witchcraft I have used.

The sun was just about to slip below the rim of the desert. As he looked towards it there was a brilliant green flash. When Clive had seen it before, he had thought he must be dreaming, but others had seen it too.

The green flash is a common phenomenon and is real (not illusory), seen at sunrise and sunset, when some part of the Sun suddenly changes colour, from red or orange to green or blue. The word 'flash' refers to the sudden appearance and brief duration of this green colour, which usually lasts only a second or two at moderate latitudes. It was thought to be a modern phenomenon but was observed and noted by the ancient Egyptians, and is frequently observed in Libya and Egypt).

In January 1985 Clive Caldwell received a letter from the brother of one of the pilots he had shot down nearly half a century before. His name was August Graf von Kageneck, and on Christmas Eve 1941 his younger brother Erbo had been flying a Messerschmitt Bf. 109 near Derna in Libya. Clive had forced him down in the desert.

It was an extraordinary victory. The Germans were flying higher than the Australians but Clive pulled his aircraft up into a steep climb firing all the way. One of his bullets penetrated the cockpit, severely wounding Erbo, who still managed to force land his aircraft in the desert. Erbo was an ace credited with 69 kills, and a winner of the Knight's Cross.

Eighteen days later, Erbo died of his injuries in a Luftwaffe hospital in Naples. Before he died he wrote to his parents: 'On the way home someone shot me properly from below.'

In his letter to Clive, Erbo's brother wrote:

> I have not the slightest hostile feeling for you. On the
> contrary we are all glad that this awful slaughter has come
> to an end—more than 40 years now.
>
> But to find almost four and half decades later the person
> who was responsible for the death of my brother is a strange
> hazard only possible by the very special character of the
> individual fighting in the air.
>
> We other poor earthworms (I was with the Panzers in
> Russia) certainly never knew and will never know who shot
> us and whom we shot.

Taking the long way home

By the time Clive left the desert he had shot down 20 and a half aircraft, and flown 550 hours on operations. All of his victories were while flying the Tomahawk or the Kittyhawk, but newer fighters were starting to appear, and Clive wanted a chance to fly them.

After the Japanese raided Darwin, the Australian government was insistent that Clive come home, even though the RAF were keen to retain his services. Clive saw no sense in returning to an air force that had no modern fighter aircraft; he wanted to stay where the action was.

He would eventually return. But first he was ordered to report to England. It was considered too dangerous to fly directly via the Mediterranean so Clive went the long way round, via West Africa, the Caribbean, the United States and Canada, and it was seventeen days before he arrived.

These were long boring flights. The aircraft usually

departed at dawn and would spend all day in the air. A big
Boeing Clipper flying boat took him from Heliopolis in Egypt
to Khartoum in the Sudan, then to Kano and Lagos in
Nigeria, and Accra in the Gold Coast (Ghana). From there
they flew to Liberia, Sierra Leone, Natal and Belem in Brazil,
Port of Spain, Trinidad, Boringuin in Puerto Rico, and finally
to Washington D.C. The last leg was from Montreal to
Prestwick in Scotland arriving on 29 May 1942.

By June he was back in the air, commanding the RAF's
famous Kenley Wing just south of London. During the Battle
of Britain two years earlier, Kenley had been in a front row
seat and had been heavily bombed by the Luftwaffe. But now
the airfield was on the offensive, and its Spitfires were
ranging far and wide over France looking for targets of
opportunity.

Clive relished ground attack work—the idea of taking the
battle to the enemy. On 2 July he added a locomotive to his
list of kills. His logbook records: 'One steam train (passenger)
near St. Omer. Engine and carriages. Three runs.'

Clive was not about to tell the RAF how it should have
fought the Battle of Britain, but he had his own theories. With
the advantage of defensive radar, the RAF could always see
bombers forming up over France prior to crossing the English
Channel. Rather than waiting for them to cross the coastline,
Clive believed in taking the fighters across to France and
meeting them on their ground:

> If we'd have sent the squadron over, they would have had to
> get their fighters off to protect the bombers. You could have

been like a hawk among the pigeons. They couldn't put a raid on could they? Or they'd have to come without fighters.

That's what I would have thought. Go and bloody well get into them, which is what we used to do in the desert with low level strafing.

Clive relished his time in England but it was to last little more than a month. By 29 July he was back in the United States, being told to report to Lord Halifax, the British Ambassador in Washington. Clive enjoyed celebrity status in America and was feted on the cocktail party circuit, even being presented to President Roosevelt.

Clive was the highest-scoring Commonwealth fighter pilot to have flown Curtiss aeroplanes. As he had made good use of the P 40s they had built he was invited to address the workers at the Curtiss aircraft factory. He told them: 'A man has every right to have faith in himself. If he hasn't he can't expect it from others.'

Clive toured the assembly plant and was asked to fly the newest model of the Kittyhawk, the P 40F.

This aircraft powered with the Packard-made Merlin engine is a marked improvement on the P 40E Kittyhawk by virtue of the fact that the engine has a two-speed supercharger, a higher brake horsepower engine and performs better at all heights.

I was told by Mr. Wright that tests are being carried out with a view to lightening the overall weight of the fuselage of this machine which should result, of course, in increased performance. It is still however well behind our Spitfire in all round performance.

It had been arranged that he would fly five other American fighters on offer to Australia, and assess their potential. These were the North American P 51 Mustang, the Republic P 47 Thunderbolt, the Lockheed P 38 Lightning, the Bell P 39 Airacobra, and the Chance Vought Corsair.

In America he met a kindred spirit in the aircraft designer, Alexander Seversky, whose work on an earlier type, the Lancer, led to one of the heaviest fighters of World War II, the Thunderbolt.

He was very disappointed in the Thunderbolt but I thought it was a bloody good aeroplane. He had designed it to weigh 7400 pounds and it weighed about 15 000 pounds.

Clive was impressed with Seversky's book, *Victory Through Air Power:*

. . . considering it was written six years before the war, pointing out how important air power would be in the coming war and particularly the need to have fighter cover. This is where we were a bit wrong in England. We had the defence only and could not escort our bombers so they had to bomb at night, which isn't as good because you can't get formation bombing at night, can you?

Testing the capabilities of new aircraft was exhilarating, and Clive marvelled at the way fighter technology had advanced in just four years. Of the aircraft he flew he liked the Mustang and the Thunderbolt best. The original Mustang had been designed in the summer of 1940 to meet a request by the British Purchasing Commission. Fitted with an American Allison engine similar to that installed in the Kittyhawk, its performance was lacklustre at altitude.

It was only when it was fitted with a Packard-built Rolls Royce Merlin that the Mustang came into its own as the pre-eminent long range escort fighter of World War II. Australia was a big country, and the Mustang had a 1000-mile range. Unfortunately the aircraft was still being tested when Clive flew it and would not enter quantity production until 1943. He thought the Mustang was the aircraft that best fitted the bill, but the RAAF was not to receive them until the end of the war, and later they were to be manufactured under license.

Instead of any of these machines, Australia was to receive the Spitfire.

Another incident relieved the routine flight test program. Clive agreed to go on a test flight in a large Curtiss C 46 Commando freight plane. The flight was only supposed to last for half an hour, with Clive sitting in the right hand seat as second pilot. But when the plane came in to land, the crew discovered that the hydraulic lines to the undercarriage had fractured and the landing gear could not be locked or pumped fully down. Clive had to take over the controls, while Herbert Fisher, the chief pilot, clambered down below the floorboards to see if he could could lower the wheels manually. The plane circled around for eight hours to use up fuel before Fisher decided to attempt a belly landing at the Curtiss Wright aerodrome in Buffalo. The big aircraft skidded along the runway on its engine nacelles in a shower of sparks and came to a halt relatively undamaged. There were no casualties and afterwards the passengers posed for a celebratory photograph.

Compared with many of the crash landings that Clive had experienced it was a piece of cake.

Later he received a letter from Burdette S. Wright, the vice-president of the Curtiss Wright Corporation:

My dear Caldwell:

This is to certify the eight hours of exposure afforded you as co-pilot in the Curtiss Commando type of aircraft under the tutelage and frequently (while he was in the basement) physically over Herbert Fisher, chief pilot on 6th August 1942 in the immediate vicinity of the Buffalo (New York) Municipal Airport.

I feel sure that you have confidence in flying and landing this type of aircraft (wheels up or wheels down). Further we all enjoyed your short stay in Buffalo (sorry you had to spend so much of it in the air).

Clive was next to visit the Allison engine plant in Indianapolis but, because of the lengthy flight in the Commando, he missed the train. Curtiss arranged a plane to fly him there. At Indianapolis, Clive did the usual factory tour, and had meetings with members of the engineering and design teams.

Clive had no complaints about the Allison engine; in fact it had saved his life on more than one occasion; but as tactfully as he could he told the Americans about the great strides being made in engine development by the Germans and the British.

I was again interested to find that some surprise was evidenced at the actual horsepower and performance of the Messerschmitt Bf. 109 and the Focke Wulf 190. Also, the gathering seemed slightly incredulous of the performance of the late model Spitfires. I was, however, very impressed by what I had seen of the efficiency of the plants, and the research work being done to produce engines with a higher horsepower rating and increased operational efficiency.

Clive's easy going laconic manner made him popular with the Americans and, because he had been serving in a Royal Air Force squadron, he was frequently invited to social functions organised by the British community. In Los Angeles he was wined and dined at the Beverly Hills home of Nigel Bruce, the English actor who played Watson in the Sherlock Holmes movies. He met a number of Hollywood celebrities, including Mary Pickford, the silent movie star and one of the founders of United Artists.

In September, Clive caught another Boeing Clipper from San Francisco to Hawaii, then got a lift on a B 17 bomber to Christmas Island, Canton Island, Noumea, Fiji and finally Brisbane.

After the excitement of the desert, Clive was now assigned to the role he had initially sought to avoid. He knew that there he could collect information about the Japanese, their aircraft and their techniques. Although reluctant to be there himself, Clive believed that Group Captain Peter Jeffrey had set up a very fine training unit at Mildura, the dry, fruit-growing district in northern Victoria. Clive's job at the Operational Training Unit of RAAF Mildura was to teach novice pilots the business of shooting aircraft down.

Not everybody was enamoured of Clive's abrasive style. Wing Commander Dick Cresswell had known him before he had gone to North Africa.

We called him the biggest con-man the air force ever had. He got everyone to help him out.

A lot of the guys who flew with Caldwell weren't very impressed with him at all.

As an individual pilot he was very good. As a leader, useless. A poor leader. A lot of people were scared of him. He was older than most of us—eight or nine years older than me. He was over the age limit when he tried to get into the air force. But he was an individual pilot.

Once at Mildura at Fighter OTU I came down as chief flying instructor and who was the chief instructor?— Caldwell. We never spoke for the five months we were there.

He could fly any aircraft but so could I. He avoided me like the bloody plague. I didn't trust him. I wouldn't trust him as far as I could see him. In the sense that he looked after himself rather than the squadron's pilots.

Clive was now asked to test an Australian aircraft, the Boomerang.

It had been designed by Fred David, a German Jew who had made Australia his home after working in both the German and Japanese aircraft industries. At the outbreak of the war, Australia had no modern fighter aircraft, despite the fact that it had sought to buy them from Britain and Japan.

David was given the job of designing a fighter around the biggest engine then available, the 1200 horsepower Pratt and Whitney Wasp. The Boomerang was designed and built in only three months—by any definition an astonishing feat for Australia's fledgling aircraft industry.

When Clive flew the aircraft he was not impressed.

George Jones was very angry at my condemnation of the aircraft as a fighter and at what he regarded as a cheap attempt to denigrate our local war effort. He demanded that I rewrite my report.

I refused but I did delete the final paragraph, ie 'The most noticeable thing about the Boomerang is that in direct contrast to its name its unlikelihood of return if it ever met any enemy aircraft!!'

Clive was not the only pilot to criticise the shortcomings of the Boomerang. The pilots of No 2 Operational training unit made the following conclusions:

General handling characteristics of the aircraft: poor.

All-round performance in comparison with enemy fighter aircraft types: extremely poor.

All-round performance in comparison with other Allied fighter aircraft: is also poor.

The recommendation was that the Boomerang be used as a trainer or as a night fighter. But the little panic fighter did have something going for it—its extreme manoeuvrability and its ability to be used low down as a sort of flying bulldozer. In New Guinea it was used in the army cooperation role for marking targets and attacking enemy positions. And even Clive would have to admit that the Boomerang proved that Australia could at least design and build its own aircraft.

New command

Clive Caldwell had missed out on commanding his elite Spitfire squadron in England. But back in Australia, after the time in Mildura, he was placed in command of three Spitfire squadrons, two of them RAAF and one RAF. The RAAF squadrons No 452 and 457 had been formed in England in April and June 1941 whereas the RAF's No 54 squadron had a long history dating back to 1916. The three squadrons formed what became known as the No 1 Fighter Wing or the Churchill Wing.

The RAF's 54 Squadron had been in action since the outbreak of the war, and had claimed its first victory over the Luftwaffe in February 1940. Early in the war the squadron maintained air cover over convoys in the Thames Estuary, and helped to cover the evacuation of the British Expeditionary Force from Dunkirk. Later based at Hornchurch, it was in the front row of the Battle of Britain.

A number of high scoring pilots, like Al Deere the New

Zealander, had been with the squadron in England, but the squadron had lost 21 of its most experienced pilots in the Battle of Britain, and by 1941 had been moved to Yorkshire for a rest.

Most of the current 54 Squadron personnel were new to air fighting, with the exception of the two flight commanders, Flight Lieutenants Bob Foster and Robin Norwood. The commanding officer, Squadron Leader Eric George Gibbs, had flown Ansons in a general reconnaissance squadron.

Of the 95 pilots in the wing, only six had any experience, 37 had some combat background and the rest were new to operations. It was Clive's job to lick them into shape.

The first raid on Darwin in February 1942 had been an enormous shock to Australians, but that had been only the beginning. Since then there had been another 50 raids, and the Japanese were stepping up their attacks, making raids by day and night. At first the only fighter aircraft that could meet the Japanese on anything like equal terms were the P 40s flown by the American pilots of the 33rd Pursuit group, but they had been seriously mauled in the first raid and ten aircraft had been lost. Now they had been reinforced by Australians—the RAAF Kittyhawks of 77 and 76 Squadrons.

By January 1943, 70 Spitfires and more than 700 ground staff had moved up to Darwin, occupying the three new strips carved out of the bush at Strauss and Livingstone.

Australia received only two versions of the Spitfire, the Mark V and the Mark VIII and, for security reasons, the aircraft became known by the curious name of the Capstan, which was also a brand of cigarette. The Merlin engines, meanwhile, were known as Marvels.

The first batch of aircraft ordered for Australia was diverted instead to the Desert Air Force, but then the first six of 245 Spitfire Vs to carry RAAF colours arrived by ship in Melbourne. They were taken to Laverton to be assembled by clerks and bricklayers.

During the six week sea journey it would have been difficult to disguise the fact that the ships were carrying aircraft and there would have been plenty of spies en route. Japanese intelligence had got wind of the Capstans' arrival in Australia, and Radio Tokyo announced that whether they were filter-tipped or plain, they would burn just the same!

On 4 March the BBC made it official, announcing that Spitfires had arrived in the South-West Pacific. Now it was no longer a secret, the aeroplane received all the attendant publicity of an operatic diva. It was the aeroplane that had saved Britain in her hour of need. Now it would save Australia. The newsreels showed Australia's Minister for External Affairs, 'Doc' Evatt, shaking hands with Spitfire pilots in England, and spirited flying displays were given at Laverton and Richmond.

There are probably more words written about the Spitfire than any other aircraft in the history of aviation, and with good reason. Even after 70 years it is still one of the best looking aeroplanes of all time. It first flew in 1936, and was still in service with many air forces more than 20 years later.

The Spitfire was produced in huge numbers—22 000 aircraft and 22 different marks. It was a fine aircraft, but whether it was the aircraft to defend a country the size of

Australia is open to debate. It was developed as a defensive fighter to protect the British Isles and, as such, could not stay in the air for very long. Probably, if it had been immediately available, the Mustang might have been more appropriate; but in 1943 most of those produced were going to the Americans and the British.

The Spitfire's great virtue in the air had been its ability to turn inside any opposing fighter. Now came an aircraft which could out-turn it in a dogfight.

The Zero.

In the late 1930s anyone who thought that the Japanese could have designed a world beating fighter aircraft would have been laughed out of court. This was a nation that produced cheap imitations of cameras, cars and radio sets. They were copiers, not innovators. Or so the Western world believed.

The Zero took its name from Japanese Naval Air Force specification Type O for a carrier-based fighter. Officially it was the Mitsubishi A 6M Zero, but many Australian pilots called it the Zeke. It was extremely light (some said with a structure which would fall apart in high G manoeuvres), highly manoeuvrable, heavily armed and it could fly nearly three times as far as the Spitfire. The Zero had first appeared in 1940 during the Japanese war against China. In one engagement, near Chungking, the Zeros shot down 27 Chinese fighters, and later they had faced Claire Chennault's American Volunteer Group in Burma.

Like the Messerschmitt in North Africa, the Zero achieved a legend of invincibility; it was the slashing sword of the samurai with which Japan would defeat all its enemies. The

Americans had received early intelligence reports about the new wonder fighter and politely filed these away without interest. But when the Zero made its appearance at Pearl Harbor, they had to take notice.

Before arriving in Darwin, Clive had studied intelligence reports about engagements between the Zero and the Kitty-hawk in Hawaii.

> It was a lot better aeroplane than people thought and a lot of the time very well flown . . . Some people thought it was like a hummingbird and it could fly backwards but I think that was exaggerated.
>
> Some of some of the stuff which had been published from Kittyhawk engagements with the Zero in Hawaii wouldn't apply to the Spitfire anyhow.

One thing was clear however—if the Spitfire got into a dogfight with the Zero, it would lose.

Darwin

The desert had been dry and dusty, Darwin was hot and wet. At first light on 25 January 1943, the Motor Vessel *Maetsuycker* tied up in Darwin harbour and the crews of the three Spitfire squadrons—pilots, flight mechanics, riggers, instrument bashers and erks—stepped onto the wharf. This was the monsoon and their arrival coincided with a tropical downpour, something they would have to get used to in the next few months.

The RAF squadron No 54 was based in Darwin itself, but the two Australian squadrons were 35 miles south. The two strips, Livingstone and Strauss, were partly hidden among the trees alongside the main road.

Both Livingstone and Strauss had been named after American pilots who had already died in the defence of Australia. There were two 5000-foot runways paved with clay, bound with gravel and covered with a coat of diesel oil.

Beyond them was a township of huts and tents, built of bush timber, hessian and tarred paper with roofs of corrugated iron.

'You expect me to land on that?' said one of the English pilots.

In England he had been used to green fields and hedge-rows. From the air the strips at Livingstone and Strauss looked like narrow gashes in the bush. This was deliberate, to make them difficult to detect from the air. When you were landing an aircraft the trees seemed uncomfortably close and the pilots always had the impression they were squeezing their aircraft between them.

The Officers' Mess, a hut with a concrete floor and a tin roof, had been left behind by the departing Americans. It was open on all sides for ventilation, and fitted out with a mess table and some benches and easy chairs looted from the Hotel Darwin by 'persons unknown'. There wasn't much in the way of creature comforts—a wind-up gramophone, packs of cards, a radio, a cribbage board, a game of checkers and a chess game. This was to be Clive Caldwell's home for the next six months.

The officers who served under him were shockingly young. They stroked their new moustaches and smoked pipes to give themselves an air of authority. Barely five years before they would have been kicking a ball around the school playground; now they had been given command of an aeroplane that was capable of 350 miles an hour. It was the nature of the job. To be a fighter pilot you needed good eyesight and quick reactions; you also had to be prepared to take risks.

Operations in the desert had been relentless; on just one

day 112 Squadron had carried out 69 sorties. In Darwin, however, the enemies were boredom, inactivity and the exhaustion of operating in a climate where in summer the humidity was often as high as 95 per cent.

In the first Darwin raid, fighters and dive bombers had been launched from the same aircraft carriers which had attacked Pearl Harbor. Now the raids were being carried out from the Japanese base at Penfui in Timor. The Japanese were playing away—to attack the Australians they had first to fly across 300 miles of water and back again. And even though the Zero could fly 1200 miles, dog-fighting used up a lot of fuel.

The Japanese had already been snooping around with reconnaissance aircraft but initially there was no sign of the fighters or bombers. The first blood went to an English pilot with 54 Squadron, Flight Lieutenant Bob Foster, who shot down a high flying Mitsubishi Dinah, not the easiest of machines to catch. The next day the Japanese sent over a second Dinah which got away. This one presumably took pictures from the air, confirming the presence of the three Spitfire squadrons.

It was now only a matter of time before the Japanese sent over their bombers, but the weather was still appalling. Jim Grant, whose job was to service the instruments in the Spitfires recorded in his diary:

Friday 26th February Weather lousy
　Saturday 27th Weather worse
　Sunday 28th Weather has deteriorated, hasn't stopped

raining for two days. No flying. Clothes damp and smell of mildew. Will have to build an ark if this continues.

Even the birds, it seemed, were walking. The Spitfire pilots consoled themselves with the fact that if they couldn't get into the air, neither could the Japanese. The boys were at a loose end. Flying Officer Ross Williams whiled away the time constructing long snakes out of Mah-Jongg tiles. Others tried to sleep, though it was difficult because they were wearing flying clothes to be prepared for action.

Great initiative was also shown by the erks—mechanics and riggers on the ground. Ron Lambert discovered that you could chill a bottle of beer by putting it in a sock and spraying it with 100 octane fuel. Others discovered that by secreting a bottle in the ammunition chutes and flying the Spitfire to 15 000 feet it could be suitably chilled, although it was ill-advised to fly any higher because the beer would freeze and the cap would blow off.

The boredom was bound to encourage practical jokers. One morning after a Japanese night raid, a squadron armaments officer was approached by a group of pilots gingerly carrying a tin. They suggested he hold it up to his ear to hear it ticking. The officer listened for a second, threw the tin into a slit trench and sent a hand grenade in after it. On inspecting the remains of the bomb he discovered he had destroyed an alarm clock and a perfectly good cake tin!

The English pilots of 45 Squadron could not believe the weather; after the rain the cloudless blue skies and the brilliant white Australian light. Their commanding officer Eric Gibbs wrote:

> It was different in England. There you sat around a fire all day, moaning to the adjutant that there wasn't enough coal, huddled up in mufflers, Irvine jackets and flying boots, reading or playing poker or reviewing the beer and blonde situation.

Some of the homesick pilots had tried to plant a garden with English pansies, chrysanthemums and dahlias and were dismayed to find they soon withered in the fierce tropical sun. At night everyone slept under mosquito nets, but these were not the only insects causing trouble. One pilot reported that his air speed indicator was not working, even though his aircraft was handling satisfactorily. An investigation of the pitot tube, which protrudes from the leading edge of the wing, showed that a wasp had built its nest there.

On most nights, dance music could be heard coming from the gramophone in the Officers' Mess but there was not a huge selection and the same record was being played over and over again. One night the music stopped abruptly and Jim Grant heard the sound of gunfire. Clive Caldwell was throwing the records into the air and shooting them with his revolver.

By 2 March 1943 the weather had improved, and the Wing did not have to wait long to see some action. Clive was now to engage the legendary Zero for the first time.

Further south from Livingstone was the base at Coomalie

Creek, which was occupied by the Beaufighters of 31 Squadron. Earlier in the year the Beaufighters had flown across the Timor Sea to attack the Japanese base at Penfui in Timor. Now, the Japanese were repaying the compliment.

Unlike the war in the desert, the Australians had radar to warn them of incoming aircraft even if it was not always 100 per cent accurate. At three minutes to two in the afternoon the scope showed two groups of aircraft 120 miles north-west of Darwin both converging on Coomalie Creek.

Bandits at angels one five.

The squadrons did not even have a bell or a siren to warn them of the approaching enemy. Instead, an old truck wheel had been suspended from a tree, and was beaten with a piece of metal.

Ding! Ding! Ding!

. . . Scramble!

Clive raced towards his aircraft, grabbing his parachute from the end of the wing. The mechanic had already started the engine. Strap in, turn on the oxygen, see that the mechanic removes the pitot tube cover, trolley accumulator unplugged, hand your valuables to the rigger in case you don't come back, and they have to be sent on to your next of kin.

In five minutes the Spitfires were at 15 000 feet but there was no sign of the Japanese. Unknown to Clive the Zeros had already strafed Coomalie Creek, but they were flying so low the radar operators could not find them. The Spitfires were receiving instructions from two sets of radar—one operated by the Air Force the other by the Army anti-aircraft gunners. The Army's was considered to be better.

Then in his headset Clive heard: 'White section proceed to Banjo angels one five' (Banjo was the codename for Cape Paterson, as per the Australian poet). By now Clive had been airborne for an hour and a quarter, and had only 20 minutes fuel left by the time he saw the raiders.

To engage in combat now, with the engine in high revs and the supercharger engaged, would use up his remaining fuel very rapidly. Three light bombers escorted by nine Zeros were now directly above him and heading for home. They had the height and the advantage.

Clive then did an extraordinary thing. He deliberately ordered his formation to fly under the Zeros to tempt them down. The Japanese now had three alternatives, as Clive said:

> They must either turn on their backs and attack vertically downwards, a difficult shot and easily avoided, loop fully as they are credited with doing so freely thus coming up behind us or turning and losing height to come in behind us. Any attack from them must be preceded by such manoeuvres as to give us sufficient warning to meet it.

Clive dived to attack, and then pulled the Spitfire up in a wide climbing turn, followed by the rest of the formation. The Japanese seemed fazed by this, but Clive reasoned they had been in the air for two hours and they still had to get home. They did not seem that keen to fight.

Clive decided to provoke them into a fight, and made a

diving head on attack on one of the Zeros. Before it was close enough for Clive to fire, it broke downwards and dived away. Before now Clive had only seen photographs of the A 6M Zero.

Now here it was, large as life, and over Australia, dark green with bright red discs on the wing and fuselage, a black disc around its big radial motor and an intermittent yellow flash bursting from the engine mounted cannon.

> I observed several Zekes (Zeros) fire on me and took necessary action; others seemed not to have fired but the shooting was bad despite liberal use of tracer and the attempts at correcting aim were poor.

Now it was time to see how the Spitfire would turn with the Zero. Clive was doing about 260 miles an hour when he threw the aircraft into a tight turn. The Zero followed, but did not get dangerously close, and Clive had no trouble losing him.

In the Royal Automobile Club in George Street, Sydney, Clive is reliving it all. It seems that the Zeros fly off the wall and around the crystal chandeliers, the sound of cannon fire reverberates off the wooden panels.

> So we had no time to do much about this because of shortage of fuel and we're going away anyhow so wherever we're going we've got to get back. So, in order to get straight in to see what we could do, we went in under the top cover. Here, where it's easy to see them if they come down, there's no trick in this one. They can't do much to

you with you seeing them. So we made a simulated head-on attack across to the other fighters which drew them over. We dived under them and onto the little bomber formation then came back up. And I thought, well, now there's a golden opportunity to see how we turn with the Zero.

And at that height we had the advantage, but not to turn keep the speed down the same as the Messerschmitts did with the Hurricanes. That's what you do if you've got the advantage of height and speed—retain the advantage, that's what you do—just keep pecking at 'em. What do they call it when eagles do it? I've forgotten. That's the way they do it—past fast—go back to the height then do it again.

Anyway that came out right. I wrote about two pages of this sort of stuff at that time for general guidance and also for the Fighter OTU at Mildura where Group Captain Peter Jeffrey was commander.

Wally Walters called up and said, 'There are a couple near me now approaching me.' I said, 'I think I see them alright.' I started to turn on one of them. As soon as I got down to about 180 miles an hour he was quite clearly going to be far superior in the turn. To get away from him I put the kite in a very steep turn and rolled inside the turn.

I couldn't reverse it underneath because I would have stalled it but went down and turned right and he came after me. We were going pretty fast by the time we came out of this. And he was not turning as well in the dive to the right as I was. Anyway, I got back up a little height. The whole thing only took about four and a half minutes, and during this time I got quite a bit of information about the Zero and decided that there was no way we would would ever get involved in dog-fighting Zeros.

We must have height which we could get. The Spitfire Mark V was able to gain height every bit as fast as a Zero but not at quite as steep an angle. We were going to height at a slightly lesser angle but the Spitfire was a little faster to a greater height to 36 000 feet; they're struggling at 32 000 feet.

The whole engagement lasted only eight minutes, and Clive went on to shoot down a Zero and one of the light bombers, a Kate.

First blood to the Spitfire. The Zero was not invincible!

I observed Zekes to loop to half roll and to fire while on their backs, which, though interesting as a spectacle seemed profitless in dog-fighting.

Clive thought the Spitfire the better aircraft despite the fact that the Zeros had the upper hand.

I regard the Spitfire as a superior aircraft generally, though less manoeuvrable at low speeds. In straight and level flight, and in the dive, the Spitfire appears faster.

On 15 March, 24 bombers and 25 fighters appeared over Darwin, this time heading for the oil storage tanks. Once again the Japanese had the advantage of height, and the pilots of the 27 Spitfires which intercepted them pushed their machines to the limit to get up to them.

The engagement was right over the centre of town, so the anti-aircraft gunners were told not to open fire. Cliff Taylor, a gunner with the Fannie Bay battery, had a front row seat:

> They clashed right overhead. Dog-fights ranged from about 25 000 feet to almost ground level, with some of the Spits going straight at the bombers. Planes wheeling, milling, machine guns, cannon fire, planes on fire, pilots bailing out, men dying—it's hard to imagine that this happened in Australia. I shall never forget the air battles.

The smoke of battle hung over the town for the best part of an hour. Six Japanese fighters were destroyed with nine probables and five damaged. Four Spitfires were lost and three pilots killed, including the commanding officer of 452 Squadron, Ray Thorold-Smith, a medical student from Manly and one of Caldwell's closest friends.

Clive had been off the base receiving medical treatment for his leg wound when the raid developed, so he ordered Thorold-Smith to lead the wing until he could get into the air himself. Thorold-Smith had been on night-flying operations and was returning to the strip at Strauss with four other Spitfires. Despite the fact his pilots were dog-tired, he turned them around and climbed to engage the bombers.

The trouble started when two of the five pilots reported they were low on oxygen, and had to return to base. Thorold-Smith called 'Tally Ho' and announced he was going to attack but nothing was seen or heard from him again. Later the next afternoon an eye-witness reported that a Spitfire had been observed crashing into the water near Flagstaff Hill. Although a search was mounted, no wreckage was found and his body was never recovered.

Thorold-Smith was posted as: 'Missing Enemy Action Cause Unknown'.

This was a serious blow to Clive. As well as a good friend, Thorold-Smith was a popular leader and an experienced pilot with seven kills under his belt, most of them in Europe. He could ill afford to lose him.

Although Clive was not there, his report of the episode is extremely critical of the British squadron. Thorold-Smith had instructed 54 Squadron to climb above him while he attacked the bombers. This they failed to do:

No 54 Squadron covering above did not fly the battle formation they had been trained to do, but were line astern to each other and were jumped out of the sun losing two aircraft shot down, Sergeant Varney and Sergeant Cooper. Also, they admit that in addition they were all looking towards the bombers. Therefore, being in trouble themselves, they were unable to give the expected cover to Squadron Leader Smith and his sections below them.

After the loss of Thorold-Smith, Clive told the Englishman, Squadron Leader Gibbs, that he would be court martialled if he again disobeyed a command. This would have been a bitter pill for Gibbs to swallow. Gibbs might only have been a squadron leader, but he was a permanent officer in the Royal Air Force, not a graduate of the Empire Air Training Scheme.

We will never know for sure what happened to Ray Thorold-Smith. There was some suggestion that he too had run low on oxygen which had produced a feeling of euphoria and affected his judgment. He had 750 flying hours to his credit, 500 of them on Spitfires.

Forty-three years later, in 1983, his aeroplane was found in the mud on the western reaches of Darwin Harbour. The propeller was still set in coarse pitch, which suggests that he was not alert when he ditched the aircraft.

When Japanese aircraft were shot down, more of them came down in the water than on land, so rarely did the Spitfire pilots of Number 1 Fighter Wing come face to face with the men they had destroyed.

One exception was the Dinah reconnaissance aircraft shot down by Squadron Leader Ken James on 18 July. Ken had intercepted the aircraft at 26 000 feet. He closed to 250 yards and fired a two second burst from line astern seeing his shells hit the port engine. The aircraft began to spin then, when it was 5000 feet from the ground, it blew up.

The Dinah had crashed near Adelaide River Station so three officers set off in a jeep from Livingstone to see if they could find it. The party spent two hot uncomfortable days in the bush before they located the wreck with the help of Aboriginal trackers.

The aircraft was spread all over the bush, and only the forward position of the pilot's nacelle was recognisable. The Dinah gave the impression of being extremely light and appeared either to be new or in immaculate condition, there being no oil slicks on what remained of the fuselage. The party found eight fuel tanks in the wing. No wonder the Dinah could fly so far and so fast!

The bodies of the two airmen were found nearby. The pilot wore a parachute and harness, and appeared to have tried to bail out at very low altitude. But the shroud lines had been torn from the canopy, possibly caused by the chute hitting a tree. There was a hole in his shoulder and both his left leg and right arm were broken.

The second body had already been pecked at by crows and the face was barely recognisable. He wore no parachute and his boots were missing but, curiously, two khaki socks were found lying together next to his naked feet, which suggested he may have survived the crash. Neither of the Japanese airmen wore any sort of identification. Nearby they found the aircraft's camera, an American Fairchild F 24, containing two spools of film.

The crew was later identified as Captain Shunji Sasaki and Lieutenant Akira Eguchi of the 70th Direct Command Squadron of the Japanese Army Air Force. The following day they were buried in shallow graves.

A severe reverse

There were no raids at all in April and the pilots relieved the boredom by practising their shooting and battle tactics. Clive endlessly lectured his pilots about the technique of shadow shooting which he had first used in the desert. Now they practised south of Darwin over the muddy waters of Bynoe Bay, once again aiming ahead of the shadow of the aircraft on the water.

But after the raid on 2 May they were astonished to read that they had suffered a 'severe reverse'.

On 6 May the *Nippon Times* reported:

Although the anti-Axis headquarters merely announced that the losses their air units suffered in aerial combats with the Japanese air force were serious . . . the results gained by the Japanese air units have apparently given a severe jolt to the Australians.

The question of why Spitfires, considered by the anti-Axis camp to be the best fighter plane in the world, failed to show their power in air combats in the 2 May raid has become the centre of much heated discussion in Australia.

SPITFIRES DOWN OVER DARWIN. LOSSES HEAVY BUT MOST PILOTS SAFE

The *Daily Telegraph* in Sydney said about the raids:

Tokyo official radio claimed last night that 21 Allied fighters were shot down by Japanese navy planes in Sunday's raid on Darwin. The radio added that all the Japanese planes returned after heavily damaging Darwin military installations.

A GHQ official spokesman last night said that the Tokyo claim was greatly exaggerated. Earlier the official communique on the raid had stated that our losses were 'heavy'. Hugh Dash, *Daily Telegraph* war correspondent, points out that this is the first time in 386 communiques issued from General MacArthur's headquarters that the word 'heavy' has been used to describe our air combat casualties.

In previous communiques our air losses were referred to as 'moderate', 'slight' or 'negligible'. 'The majority of the Spitfire pilots are safe,' states an official announcement issued last night.

Dash says it is possible that Jap Army pilots were drafted for this special attack on Darwin. Japan's Army pilots are easily the best of enemy air personnel.

Reports of the battle received to date do not throw conclusive light on reasons for the Spitfire losses.

The *Sun* had a similar headline:

Allan W. Dawes, the *Sun's* war correspondent, wrote:

Examinations of rescued pilots who fought the Jap raiders over Darwin on Sunday reveal that bad weather was responsible for our heavy losses. After the engagement had been broken off far out to sea with our forces in pursuit of the fleeing enemy, head winds developed and steadily increased in violence.

In coping with these a number of our aircraft were forced down. In actual combat though outnumbered, our forces were not only successful in diverting the enemy's main bombing attack—perhaps the most significant achievement—but inflicted far heavier damage on his fighters than he was able to do to ours.

Nonsense said Caldwell.

The headlines in the press suggested that the aircraft had been lost because of enemy action. The newspapers were sent up to us from the south from Sydney and Melbourne. Spitfires thrashed by Japanese. Zeros beat the devil out of the Spits.

This is the standard Australian attitude. Cut them down, don't try harder yourself just bring everyone else down. This had an adverse affect on the pilots and the crews generally.

I also had severe criticism from the chief of the air staff, Air Marshal George Jones. One would have thought he could have waited for something other than press reports.

So what happened on that Sunday morning? Whatever Allan Dawes had written, there was nothing wrong with the weather. Clive's combat report notes that it was bright and clear, the ceiling and visibility were unlimited, with a wind speed of only three and half knots from west-north-west.

The three Spitfire squadrons had been scrambled at 9.40 am and were directed by the ground controllers towards a formation of 20 Japanese bombers to the north of Darwin. Clive's eyes scanned backwards and forwards across the sky, and every ten seconds checked the rear view mirror above the canopy.

As he looked down on the white caps flecking the blue ocean he reflected on how very different this was to the air battles of the Western Desert. That had been a relatively clean war fought in a wasteland between two combatants; no civilians had been involved.

But this was different; his homeland was being attacked by invaders and civilians had been killed, 250 of them. He gritted his teeth.

Where were the bastards?
There they are!

They were high . . . the bombers at 25 000 feet and the fighter escort maybe as high as 30 000 feet.

At maximum boost it should have taken the Spitfires fifteen minutes to get to 30 000 feet, but some of the engines were not performing well, and two aircraft had to return to base. The engines had to be changed after every 240 hours and some of them were well past that.

The 31 remaining Spitfires were still below the bombers as they crossed the harbour. Clive knew he could not attack without exposing his flight to the Zeros patrolling up above. Not far below were the muddy waters of Bynoe Bay where he had taught them how to shadow shoot. Maybe he was getting too old for this sort of thing. Maybe he would make a mistake . . .

The bombers started their bombing run and dropped most of their bombs in a line close to the RAAF base and then turned right and headed for home.

By now, Clive's fighters had reached 32 500 feet and, with the sun behind them they were in a better position to attack. But the battle was moving further out to sea and fuel was running low. One by one, Spitfires were pulling out of the fight with mechanical problems. Already Sergeants Fox and Cavanagh had dropped out with engine trouble.

These were quickly followed by Flying Officer Ian Mackenzie from 457 squadron whose radio had packed up and Pilot Officer Norm Robinson with a faulty oxygen supply. Shortly afterwards, Squadron Leader Ron MacDonald of 452 Squadron found that both of his cannon had jammed. Then Flight Sergeant Ross Stagg and Flight Sergeant Bill Hardwick suffered engine failures because of a faulty constant speed unit. And so it went on.

Over the radio Clive calmly spoke to his pilots and directed them into the best position to attack. On the ground the mechanics listened in to the conversation on the headset of a parked Spitfire. The inexperienced pilots were keen to draw blood but enthusiasm sometimes swayed judgment. Clive made it all sound like he was marshalling a cricket team to take the field on a lazy Saturday afternoon.

White three close up; turning to port now; I am engaging the enemy; Tally Ho.

Ten minutes into the fight Caldwell had warned all the pilots to check their fuel and if it was low to return to base.

As we are taking the Japanese on out to sea I call to all the pilots to say that are to disengage to reduce to economic settings as soon as their reading on the lower tank is 30 gallons left and proceed on the course home which we gave them —110 degrees. Then told Fighter Control they were to repeat this instruction at two minute intervals which they did four or five times. Two very pleasant fellows died soon after this.

In the back of the Betty bomber, Petty Officer Sieji Tajiri was very cold. He had been in the air for two hours and was grateful to have safely flown over the Timor Sea, but crossing the enemy coastline, his stomach tightened into a knot. Why have we come to this place? he asked in his mind to his dead mother. She had lived in the Kyocera prefecture, famous for its ceramics, and had not been that keen on his joining the Navy.

What was this drab country with its lifeless trees and endless tracks of sand going nowhere? Where were the neat temples and cherry trees? Admiral Fuchida had told them to attack this country but it was so big. Did people live in this wasteland? The Australians were big men like sweaty oxen, but they fought like madmen.

A small aeroplane appeared as if from nowhere in the perspex glasshouse at the front of the Betty. It was getting larger, but there was no sound. There were white flashes, and bright burning projectiles skidding around his feet, bouncing off the sides of the aluminium tube which proved to be his coffin. Something hit him in the chest.

On this day, only three of the Spitfire pilots, including Clive, had any previous experience against escorted enemy bombers. Clive said:

> This general lack of experience has in no way affected the keenness of the pilots, whose moral fibre standards are of a high order. On the contrary, several of these inexperienced pilots were led away by their keenness and the natural excitement of their first combat to the extent of forgetting both time, fuel and their way home despite adequate and repeated warnings. As a direct result of this, four Spitfires were lost.

Fourteen Spitfires did not return to their bases that day, but most of them had been lost either because of mechanical problems or because they had run out of fuel. Three pilots were posted missing. In the profit margin, the three squadrons had accounted for eighteen Japanese aircraft—five fighters and two bombers and eleven probables or damaged. It was scarcely a severe reverse, but they had lost a lot of aircraft. The surviving Spitfires returned to the strip with the wind whistling in their gun ports; a sign to the ground crews that they had at least fired their guns.

But what of those who had not returned? Ross Stagg and Bill Hardwick had baled out and taken to their dinghies. Bill was rescued the same day but Ross was posted missing. Ross's survival in the crocodile-infested swamp was an amazing feat of endurance. He made it ashore and spent the next two weeks trying to find his way out of the salt flats that fringed Fog Bay. He was only about 60 miles away from base but the terrain was nearly impassable. Finally, exhausted and starving and maddened by insect bites, Ross made it to the banks of the Finniss River and was rescued by an itinerant prospector.

Flight Lieutenant Makin's aircraft ran out of petrol. He was heading back to Darwin with a fuel gauge that showed only ten gallons left when the engine stopped. He made a successful forced landing on a beach near Point Charles, and spent the next hour trying to unscrew accessories from the aircraft, his only tools being a nail file and a threepenny piece. Finally, he had to abandon his salvage efforts, because of the incoming tide. He swam ashore and spent the night at a radar station, returning to base the next day.

Two and a half thousand miles away in Melbourne, RAAF officers who flew desks rather than aeroplanes, were starting to ask questions. What was going on? Why had so many Spitfires been lost?

The career officers were looking for a scapegoat. Why had Caldwell not attacked before the Japanese had dropped their bombs?

> There was a good deal of criticism from the authorities that I'd delayed it too long. So we delayed about six minutes.
>
> However the sum total was there was no destruction on the ground. We had no aeroplanes on the ground. We took them away of course; naturally they go off to form a reserve to cover us when we come home.

Why had Clive decided to delay the attack? Certainly, climbing up immediately beneath the Zeros at only 150 miles an hour indicated airspeed, the formation would have been courting disaster.

The bombers had already dropped their bombs on land. But in Darwin harbour and over the water there was nothing of any value for them to attack.

> I wanted to inflict maximum damage with minimum losses to ourselves. Why should we not continue to delay the intercept until I could get the wing into the best possible position?

Clive was incensed by the negative publicity, and also by the fact that some of it seemed to have come from General MacArthur's HQ. Was it that General MacArthur did not want the limelight stolen by British and Australian pilots?

The Americans were also quick to criticise the wing on its losses. General George C. Kenney commander of the Fifth Air Force said:

> If they don't stop that business, I'd send them to New Guinea to serve with the Americans and learn how to fight properly.

Clive was furious, and told Kenney that they could get a replacement for him and he would happily return to Europe, from where he'd been dragged so reluctantly.

And why had Air Vice Marshal George Jones not tried to correct the various Australian press reports? Clive said:

> It might have been thought that Jones at least would have engineered for the truth before abandoning us.

Clive was also dismayed that 54 Squadron took so long to arrive at the rendezvous point at Hughes. Had the squadron been based at Sattler rather than Darwin, the interception might have been five to seven minutes earlier.

Serious problems . . .

What was becoming clear to all was that the Spitfires had some serious technical problems: with their engines, with their guns and with their propellers.

The Spitfire engine was cooled by a mixture of 70 per cent water and 30 per cent ethylene glycol. Glycol is a syrupy, sweet-tasting liquid with a high boiling point, which means that an aeroplane engine can use smaller radiators operating at higher temperatures. When the Spitfires were shipped to Australia, the glycol coolant was drained from the engines, but it was not replaced with a corrosion inhibitor, so the pipes had corroded and now leaked glycol. As the engine leaked coolant, it overheated and seized up. Sometimes, glycol would leak into the engine and clouds of white vapour would pour from the exhausts.

The second problem was the constant speed mechanism for the de Havilland hydromatic propeller. A constant speed mechanism keeps the engine operating at constant revolutions irrespective of the angle of pitch of the propeller blades. For take-off the blades are in fine pitch, but for cruising they take bigger bites of air. This meant that the blades of the propeller would go into fine pitch, the engine would dangerously over-rev to 4000 rpm and, once again, the engine would seize up.

Clive: 'The prop goes up to about 4000 revs. It doesn't do that for long. A big bang and you're on your way.'

Alex Henshaw, the famous British Spitfire test pilot, refers to the problem in his book, *Sigh For A Merlin*:

On some of the tropicalised Spitfires we had an engine rev problem of a different nature. These airscrews had the pitch range, but they suffered with control valve trouble, which caused the airscrew to stick in fine pitch if the throttle was snapped back in a steep climb and then snapped open again as the machine dived.

Clive commented, 'It happened without any violent throttle moves. Anyway for what reason would a pilot snap the throttle shut and snap it open again? Bloody silly act!'

Henshaw recalls a fellow test pilot flying over his house with the engine screaming:

The engine would over-rev and blow up, so the engine would have to be changed. I had difficulty in getting action from the manufacturers to remedy this defect as that was the first time they had heard of it, but in the end they confirmed that all the airscrews would be modified at the

Maintenance Units before delivery to the squadrons. Later, these same Spitfires were in action against the Japs and flown by Australian pilots; and in one action so many Australians were lost that I sincerely hoped to God the airscrews had not been responsible for this disaster.

Alex Henshaw is considered to be one of the greatest Spitfire pilots of all time. As chief test pilot at the factory at Castle Bromwich, he flew one in ten of all the Spitfires ever built although unlike Clive Caldwell he never flew a Spitfire in combat. In April 1980 Clive wrote to Henshaw:

I enjoyed *Sigh For A Merlin* having been too an aficionado of the Spitfire even if not of its less than best armament. On the occasion to which you refer on page 79, No 1 Fighter Wing Darwin raid No 54, five Spitfires were lost in the sea through engine failure due to excessive revs, the enemy not yet engaged. Nor was this the only instance, though the worst, and no throttle gymnastics required to induce the condition. A further excessive defect found in the Mk.Vs sent to Australia in 1942 was excessive corrosion of the glycol pipes. As a pilot of No 1 Fighter Wing during the relevant period I was familiar with the facts and in the circumstances thought you would like to know them.

In a flippant mood, Caldwell would often refer to the Spitfire dismissively 'as a pretty little sporting monoplane'. In truth, he loved to fly it, but was sometimes less than impressed by its armament. Like many pilots he thought the long range

Mustang more suited to Australian conditions, but it was a heavier aircraft and would have been inferior to the Spitfire in a dog-fight.

In his brief stay with the Kenley Wing in England, Clive had been flying the most advanced mark of Spitfire, the Mark IX, which had a bigger engine and a two-stage supercharger. So he was dismayed to find that Australia would be supplied with an earlier version, the Mark V. Not that there was anything wrong with the Mark V; in fact it was built in greater numbers than any mark of Spitfire, but considering it would be up against the Zero, it was rather like receiving last year's model.

The Spitfire was the quintessential British aeroplane. Its wonderful V12 Merlin engine was made by Rolls Royce, its tyres and brakes by Dunlop, its carburettors by SU, its instruments by Smiths, its bulletproof windscreen by Triplex Glass. But its guns were not British. The rifle calibre .303 machine guns had been designed by Colt Browning of America who had made Buffalo Bill's six shooters. They were to be built under licence by the Birmingham Small Arms company. The HS-404 20mm cannon were designed and built by Hispano Suiza, a French company which had Spanish and Swiss antecedents. These were also to be built under licence in England by the Manufacturing and Research company of Grantham. Why this most modern of aircraft was to be armed with weapons dating back to World War I is anyone's guess. A superior weapon, the Colt .5 gun, had been in production for years before the Spitfire and its sister aircraft, the Hurricane, flew. However, the deal to use .303s was maintained.

Most of the Spitfires and Hurricanes that flew in the

Battle of Britain carried eight Brownings but the pilots who flew these aircraft were keenly aware of the inadequacy of their weapons. Group Captain Peter Townsend, the famous British pilot, once described how he scored 220 strikes on a German bomber—which still managed to stagger home to its base.

The Colt was more like a small, quick-firing cannon than a machine gun. Each round fired by the Colt was four times heavier than a .303 round, and the gun could fire 850 rounds a minute. So, if Townsend's Spitfire had been armed with a battery of four of the .5 Colts, his attack would been seven times more damaging.

Caldwell thought that the positioning of the .303s on the wing of the Spitfire produced a spray of bullets, rather than a cone of fire. They spread way out so 'you don't know where they are; they're all over the bloody place'.

The .5s, Clive believed, would produce a cone of fire at 400 yards, with every gun firing into a four foot circle.

> You know where they're going. If you can bear right and you can get your deflection you know what's going to happen. Get out of the road there's going to be so much lead flying around! Bits of pilot too!

The Kittyhawks Clive had flown in the desert had been armed with .5s. Without seeking official approval, he instructed his engineers in Danish to install four .5s in one of the Mark VIII Spitfires. When news of what he had done leaked out he was summoned to Melbourne by an enraged George Jones.

Clive takes up the story:

I took the two 20 mm out and put four .5s in (the Spitfire). This caused a tremendous alarm and despondency down in Melbourne. So much so that as I'm the wing leader of the bloody wing I am ordered to proceed forthwith to Melbourne to explain myself to the Chief of the Air Staff.

What do I mean interfering with the armament on the Spitfire? There are people much more qualified than you. I said I wish you would get them to lead the bloody wing if you think there are. That's why I was brought back very reluctantly from the RAF.

It had to be re-established as it was, because if I had mine converted, everybody else was going to get theirs converted. I said everybody else is going to get it providing I could establish it would work properly. He said we have no arrangements we have no supply of .5s. I said I've got all I want from the Americans. We're doing the air defence, they'll give us anything. He said, you've made arrangements with the Americans? I said yes, Colonel Brissy, of the 132nd Bomb group. All we want. He's only too delighted. The better we are armed the better (protected) his aircraft on the ground are going to be on his airports.

Oh no, no, no. This is dreadful to think, that a mere acting wing commander should behave in such a disgraceful fashion. Have that aircraft re-established at once!

Goodbye, Caldwell. Close the door. Out!

At the end of the day, Caldwell's unauthorised modification was vindicated. In England a Spitfire with the E wing was developed with an identical armament of .5s. The guns were tested in combat by 33 Squadron RAF, who strongly supported Clive's efforts to improve the firepower of the Spitfire.

If Clive was unimpressed with the .303s Brownings, he was also critical of the 20 mm cannon which was prone to frequent stoppages. The problems started when the squadrons started receiving ammunition made at the Australian Defence Industries factory at St Mary's in Sydney. Some of the ammunition was over-size, and some was under-sized. A pilot would be lining up to shoot, and his guns would jam on one side.

Clive was of the opinion that there were saboteurs working in the munitions factory supplying oversized ammunition, although he could never prove it.

There was a great reluctance to load 20 mm ammunition into an aircraft until it had been been checked. Almost every shell had to be examined.

Bruce Watson said:

You watched the armourers go through the rounds. Of every 1000 cannon shells they inspected, you'd see a heap of 50 that they'd rejected.

They altered the guns, they altered the ammunition, they altered the bays, and they altered the feed—they made modifications which improved it, but there were things which they had to do in the field which they shouldn't have had to do. They were doing this to try and cater for the one bit of ammunition that wasn't standard.

Flying Officer Tim Goldsmith had one of those 50 dud rounds on board when he had a Mitsubishi G 4M Betty bomber in his sights. He opened fire at 250 yards range with both cannon and closed to 50 yards. But after three seconds the port cannon stopped and, shortly after that, he was shot down, probably by a Zero. The guns had been a problem. But in his report he was confident that the engagement with the enemy had been professionally conducted.

> The height and sun were absolutely in our favour, and the fact that the interception was not a smashing success seems to me to be entirely due to the individual pilot's lack of initiative and to armament failures. The attack organised by Wing Commander Caldwell was, in my opinion, 100 per cent perfect.

The reports of gun stoppages did not make good reading:

> Sqn.Ldr. James: cannon stoppage due to incorrect adjustment. Port inner Browning stoppage due to faulty ammunition.
>
> Flight/Sgt MacPherson: port gun stoppage due to empty link chute jumping out of its seating. Port inner Browning stoppage due to faulty ammunition.

Flight/Sgt Morse: outer Browning stoppage because of freezing. No gun heater pipe fitted this side of the aircraft.

W/O Briggs: port outer Browning stoppage due to ammunition jamming in tank entering ammo chute. Inner stoppage due to faulty ammo

F/O Barker: Port outer Browning stoppage due to cross feed of belt into gun.

Flight/Sgt Bruce Little: Port inner Browning stoppage due to faulty ammo.

P/O Gregory: Port inner Browning stoppage due to faulty ammo.

What was the point of flying the world's best fighter if the guns didn't work?

The so called anti-freeze for our guns it wasn't anti-freeze at all. They'd freeze solid. So you'd get yourself to 35 000 feet, get ready to fire. Nothing—no guns. This was disastrous—you get yourself into a reasonable position to intercept then find that you are reduced to about 50 per cent of your efficiency.

Darwin was a long way from anywhere, so a solution had to be found. It came in the shape of a lubricant made from glycol and soap. When word reached Melbourne that this un-orthodox solution was being employed, the creators were given a slap on the wrist. They continued using it anyway.

There were other reasons for the guns seizing up. Even in

the tropics, at 30 000 feet the temperature can be as low as minus 50 degrees Celsius. So warm air was piped from the rear of the radiator to provide heat for the guns. Unfortunately, after 20 hours flying, the light alloy pipes frequently cracked and in some cases the gun-heating pipes had never been fitted in the first place. So the guns froze.

There was one other problem with the Australian Mark V Spitfires, an ugly looking optional extra called the Vokes filter. This was a modification introduced on Spitfires flying in the dusty conditions of North Africa. Fitted over the air intake it was supposed to stop the ingestion of sand and dust into the engine.

It spoiled the lines of the aircraft by giving it a 'chin' but, more importantly, it slowed the aircraft down by maybe 30 miles an hour. Caldwell decided that the filters were not required in the Northern Territory so he had them removed and replaced with a metal panel.

Unless intelligence reports tipped them off about a raid no one ever knew for certain when the Japanese were coming. Spitfires could become unserviceable just standing on the ground, so Clive always had three personal Spitfires at his disposal in case one of them broke down.

I couldn't find myself with an aircraft that was unserviceable. One minute they are serviceable, then you go to fly them and the bloody thing's unserviceable. You can't very well take somebody out of of their aeroplane. You can't say, 'Come on Joe, hop out, I'll take I'll take your aeroplane, mine's no good'. You'd disappoint him; the other thing is you are no longer recognisable.

Air combat is a maelstrom of turning diving aircraft. As Wing Leader, Clive had to be instantly recognisable in the air so all of his Spitfires carried the white letters CR-C on the fuselage with a white band around the tail and a white spinner. He was easily identifiable as The Boss.

Clive had enough on his plate turning the No 1 Fighter Wing into an effective fighting unit without having to deal with faulty equipment. He was convinced that the squadrons had been supplied from Britain with second-hand aircraft. The record proves otherwise, but what is true is that tired replacement aircraft were sent up from training bases down south.

Most of the Spitfires supplied to No 1 Fighter Wing had only delivery mileage and had flown no more than 30 hours. Unfortunately a freighter carrying eleven Spitfires to Australia had been torpedoed in April, so in that same month the wing received no new aeroplanes.

Three clapped out Spitfires were received as replacements on 14 May. They had been supplied from the 2 Operational Training Unit in Mildura, so they had already been worked hard by novice pilots. One lasted five weeks, one six weeks, and another eleven weeks. All of them suffered glycol leaks which caused engine failures. Two pilots bailed out, one was badly burned, and one pilot force landed.

But if the Spitfires had teething problems they at least

afforded their pilots some measure of protection. The backs of the seats had a a slab of armour-plated steel to stop the pilot being shot in the back; the seat pan was also reinforced to stop a stray round from below.

The Spitfire carried two internal fuel tanks: the upper tank which was in front of the pilot, virtually in his lap, carried 48 gallons of highly volatile 100 octane fuel; the lower tank 37 gallons. The Spitfire's limited range had now been addressed with the installation of a 30 gallon long range fuel tank attached to the belly of the aircraft, which increased the range to 600 miles. This was usually jettisoned when the aircraft sighted the enemy.

They were self-sealing fuel tanks, so that if an incendiary round penetrated the tank it would not explode. The self-sealing fuel tank was lined with rubber that melted due to the kinetic energy of a bullet piercing it. The melted rubber would fill the hole created by the bullet.

The Zero fighter and the Betty bomber, the two main Japanese types which took part in raids on Northern Australia, had none of this protection.

'Defensive' features like armour-plating and self-sealing gas tanks were considered not worth the extra weight. In many cases the crew were not even supplied with parachutes. The Japanese believed in attack, not defence, and the crew were considered to be expendable. Baling out of an aircraft was not usually an option.

As experience showed, the Zero was a flying incendiary device and its dangerously lightened structure would fall to pieces when penetrated by well-aimed cannon and machine gun fire. A few good hits, and the whole aircraft would explode in a ball of flame.

The Betty, otherwise the Navy type one attack bomber, was just as vulnerable. Like the Zero it could fly a long way but it was so prone to ignite that the Allies called it the 'flying lighter'.

Evening the score

On 20 June the Spitfires were to even the score. Once again the radar showed a group of 22 bombers escorted by fighters approaching Darwin from the north-west. Clive took off to lead the wing, but his radio failed. Flying alongside his number two, Flight Lieutenant Peter Watson, he waggled his wings and indicated that he should take command.

Over Bathurst Island the three squadrons dived to attack the enemy, destroying four bombers and one fighter. The other fifteen bombers continued their bombing run unloading their ordnance on Winellie from 21 000 feet. There was havoc on the ground and people dived into their slit trenches.

It was not clear what the target was: the RAAF aerodrome, the RAAF bomb dump or one of the US Army dispersal area. Forty bombs of the daisy cutter type fell on the air force and army camps and the American dispersal area. Two huts were destroyed, and a railway truck containing 60 drums of oil set on fire. The railway line was broken in three places. After the

Betty bombers droned away nine smaller twin-engined light bombers, either Mitsubishi Dinahs or Kawasaki Lilys, made a low level attack on the airfield at only 100 feet off the deck. They had been flying so low that the radar had not picked them up. The airfield was racked with explosions and the clatter of machine gun fire. There were direct hits on one building and a hangar, and two hits on the Sergeants' Mess.

The main bomber formation was on its way home when it was attacked by 54 Squadron. This was not to be a repeat of 2 May; this time they had the altitude and they came out of the sun. Four bombers were seen to crash into the sea, and another three were dispatched by 452 Squadron. Although Clive's radio was still not functioning, he pursued the bombers out to sea, and was in turn pounced upon by several Zeros. In a running fight he downed another Zero which crashed into the sea. This had taken Clive a long way from home, so he was the last to return. It was his 25th victory.

The final score: 24 enemy aircraft destroyed or damaged, with two Spitfires lost. Three American army personnel had been killed on the ground and eleven wounded but 70 Japanese airmen lay at the bottom of the Timor Sea.

Now, belatedly, the wing received a telegram of congratulations from General Douglas MacArthur. But Clive still wasn't happy: 'In due course the real quality of the Wing emerged and MacArthur had the infernal cheek to send a personal signal of congratulations.'

One other incident had spoiled what had otherwise been a victorious day. Group Captain Wally Walters, a good friend of Clive's, had been flying that day and had downed a Zero. Clive took him on one side:

> Wally, I said to him, you let this news leak out 'cos you shot an aircraft down today. Fatal for you. Oh Christ, he said, I'm so pleased to have done it. I said to him, leave it until the end of the tour. It's all there on the record. Don't say anything about it now, let's just keep it to ourselves.

Walters was adamant that he would make his kill public. Caldwell pointed out that the top brass would take a dim view of a group captain flying on operations. That might be allowed in England in the *Real Air Force* but not in the *Royal Australian Amateur Air Force*.

> 'Oh no,' he said, 'I'd never do this—this is a great day for me.' I said, 'it'll be the end of you.' Sure enough two days later he was promoted Air Commodore. Removed.
>
> Soon as they learned that he was flying, ostensibly as a sort of Sergeant Pilot Snooks behind me, it upset them so much. You can't tell how dangerous this might be, expecting group captains to fly in the regular air force. The RAF do it all the time, of course, but not here. So he was posted within two days as I told him he would be.

Clive was right. The RAAF Command in Victoria Barracks Melbourne were quite opposed to senior officers flying combat missions.

'Marshmallow' Jones

One of the great constants in Clive Caldwell's life was a deep loathing of his superior, Air Vice Marshal George Jones. Jones has often been portrayed as a dull man lacking in leadership skills, although in reality he was hard working, capable and loyal.

Born in Rushworth, Victoria, Jones had been a motor mechanic before joining the Australian Light Horse and later the Australian Flying Corps. Like Caldwell he was a fighter ace and had shot down seven German aircraft during World War I.

Jones had his moment of glory flying Sopwith Camels. But after the war, he preferred to fly a big brown mahogany bomber. His desk. Jones was a pen pusher; he preferred administration and organisation to flying aeroplanes. When he did occasionally climb into the cockpit of an aeroplane it was to prove an embarrassment. At the RAAF base at Laverton in Victoria he had once performed aerobatics in an engineless Avro Cadet, being towed to altitude and then gliding silently to the ground. What this was supposed to demonstrate was anyone's guess.

Before the war Jones had been director of training, a role to which he was eminently suited. Then, in 1942, to everyone's astonishment, he was created Chief of the Air Staff, leap-frogging three ranks from Wing Commander to Air Vice Marshal. At least eight officers more senior to him were in line for the job, but were passed over. There was some suggestion that in selecting him the Cabinet had used the wrong list of RAAF officers, and Jones himself was said to be stunned by his appointment.

The best man was Air Vice Marshal Bill Bostock, who instead was put in charge of operations in the South-West Pacific. The relationship between Bostock and Jones fizzed and spluttered like a blown fuse, and in some ways the war became a power struggle as to who was running the air force.

With the outbreak of the World War II, George Jones had removed himself even further from operations. Historically, the RAAF had begun in Victoria in 1921. The only flying base was Point Cook and the headquarters at Victoria Barracks. But as the RAAF expanded with bases all over the country, Jones might just as well have been on another planet. He rarely left his office in Melbourne, preferring to communicate with those in the front line by letter or to summon them to Melbourne to see him. On the rare occasions when he did venture into the field to speak to his officers it was not a success.

Much later in 1944, Jones travelled to Morotai to meet Caldwell, Wilf Arthur and other senior officers to discuss their grievances. Accommodation at Morotai was minimal and

Jones held the meeting in a tent which served as the Officers' Mess. Seated at the table Jones lectured his men about their role in the war but seemed to be addressing someone in the ceiling, rarely making eye contact.

Bruce Watson was there:

> That was the only time that I actually saw him face to face and it was most unimpressive. He didn't interest anybody, I can't even remember what he talked about. It was of no real value whatsoever. But he didn't ask one question about what was going on, or about what we'd been doing—or the lack of what we'd been doing. It was mainly a dialogue about the Air Force and its construction and the support we were getting from Melbourne and so on. It was really, I think, a complete waste of an hour and a half.
>
> He would talk about the hours he spent in Avro Ansons patrolling for submarines in Port Phillip Bay and what he had done in World War I and so on, and it went down like a lead balloon, as you can imagine.

Bruce Watson noticed that while Jones was talking he had been fidgeting in his chair, and his legs seemed to be constantly moving up and down.

When the meeting was over, Caldwell cornered Watson and said: 'Come and have a look at this.'

Leading Watson over to where Jones had been sitting, he pointed to a small trench which had been dug in the sandy soil. 'Well, I don't know what that was all about,' he said with a wicked grin. 'Perhaps he was digging his own grave.'

In his little black notebook Clive wrote:

He is a masterpiece of negation.

There were very few moments at which his soldierly service to the Empire passed from actual ritual to a sense of reality. With intuitive quietness (one could discern) at the back of his eyes an acute anguish—the agony of a man aware of his total inadequacy.

Bruce Watson believes that the top brass in Melbourne were out to get Clive.

Jones had a personal vendetta towards Clive, and Clive's opinion of Jones was, of course, no better than Jones's opinion of Clive.

Hatred is an awful word to use, but I think Jones hated Clive Caldwell.

Jones thought Caldwell was arrogant. Clive thought that Jones had nothing to offer the Air Force and, in particular, nothing to offer to the fighter group.

Clive was without a doubt a tall poppy, and I think he was possibly somewhat out of control as far as they were concerned down there. He tended to ignore them when they got an opportunity to talk with him.

And I'd say that there would have been no civility whatsoever in the discussion.

After the wing's success on 20 June the pat on the back came from down south, from Melbourne:

The Commander in Chief South-West Pacific Area has directed that his congratulations are to be conveyed to the squadrons of No 1 Fighter Wing for their meritorious action against enemy raid number 55 on 20 June.

Shortly afterwards came Clive's long overdue Distinguished Service Order. The citation read:

By his coolness, skill and determination in the air he has set a most excellent example to all pilots in the wing. His skills and judgment as a leader are outstanding.

Wing Commander Caldwell has flown over 475 active operational flying hours and has carried out over 300 operational sorties. His personal score of enemy aircraft destroyed in combat has now passed 25, five of which are Japanese shot down since his return to Australia. His courage, determination, skill and his undoubtedly outstanding ability as a leader are an inspiration to his wing and worthy of the highest praise.

The decoration had come from Victoria Barracks but it probably had more to do with Bostock than Jones!

Clive's pay book for the time makes interesting reading. As a squadron leader he had been earning 31 shillings 6 pence a day; after stoppages this amounted to 26 shillings, about £9 1 shilling a week. As a group captain, his pay rose to 43 shillings 6 pence a day; after tax about £13 a week. What needled all the Empire Air Training Scheme recruits is that they were paid at a lower rate than the regular air force and yet they were in the frontline.

'Pennies and tin medals,' as Clive wrote.

Curiously Darwin was not even considered a combat area! Because of a petrified regulation which survived from the early days of the war, airmen who served there were not entitled to field service pay, freedom from taxation or to wear chevrons. So a pilot might be killed 500 miles away from Darwin but, because his base was on Australian mainland territory, he was not theoretically on overseas service.

Like Clive, many of the airmen who served in Darwin had also served overseas. So deeply did they feel the discrimination against their colleagues who had been fighting only from Australian mainland bases that, in solidarity, most of them did not wear the chevrons to which they were entitled.

There was however a spirit of good natured rivalry between the English and Australian squadrons. On one occasion after a pilot in an Australian squadron failed to shoot down a Dinah, the squadron received a bow and arrow from the English squadron, with a note attached suggesting he use it. A few weeks after, the same squadron shot down three aircraft in one day. A lone Spitfire flew over the 54 Squadron strip and dropped the bow and arrow.

A note read: 'Thanks very much. Suggest you use this next time.'

Raids decline

Between June and November 1943 the frequency of Japanese raids started to decline. It seemed to the crews that perhaps the enemy was losing interest in the fight. On 22 June the Spitfires were scrambled to intercept Betty bombers but having reached Bathurst Island the Japanese had second thoughts, turned round and flew home without making an attack.

The wing now started flying standing patrols fitting the Spitfires with even bigger 90 gallon belly tanks which enabled them to stay in the air twice as long. This meant that instead of pushing their aircraft to the limit to reach the high flying bombers, the Spitfires could patrol at high altitude.

Three modified Spitfires tried this on 25 June, and lay in wait for the Japanese. Unfortunately they didn't show up. Three days later an unusually small formation of nine bombers attacked the East Point battery at the entrance to Darwin harbour in what can only be considered as a nuisance raid.

Four daisy cutter bombs were dropped on a Public Works Department camp, and a few more on Vestey's meatworks and the Botanic Gardens. Four Spitfires were damaged, but two of those had engine problems. Once again, glycol leaks and tired engines were giving trouble.

One pilot, Flying Officer Tommy Clark, was hit in the tail and went into an inverted spin in which he encountered radial G forces which caused him to red out (before unconsciousness the pilot sees red). He managed to belly land the aircraft at Livingstone and those who went to his aid found that the whites of his eyes were indeed blood red.

There were three raids in June, one in July, three in August, two in September and the last raid, number 64, in November.

Besides the three Spitfire strips the Northern Territory was dotted with other bases. South of Livingstone and Strauss was Fenton which was occupied by the Liberator bombers of the 380th Bombardment Group of the United States Army Air Force. The big bombers had much greater range than the Beaufighters and had been raiding Japanese bases in Timor and the Celebes. Sooner or later it was inevitable that the Japanese would make a reciprocal visit.

Once again the raid was preceded by a Dinah reconnaissance aircraft sniffing around. On 30 June, two plots of aircraft were picked up 160 miles north-west of Darwin. Thirty-eight Spitfires were in the air in five minutes. Once again, the Japanese formation consisted of Bettys and Zeros; Number 54 Squadron was told to attack the bombers, 452 Squadron was to attack the fighters, 457 Squadron commanded by Clive

Caldwell was to attack the bombers from the front quarter on the port side.

But, somehow, there was a mix-up, and what had been a carefully coordinated attack turned into a near disaster. All three squadrons attacked the bombers at the same time, exposing them to a slashing attack by the Zeros. Some of the bombers meanwhile carried on to Fenton and unloaded their bombs successfully, destroying four of the huge aircraft on the ground and a dozen spare engines. Four bombers and three fighters were destroyed, with four probables and five bombers damaged.

But it was a black day for No 1 Fighter Wing. Seven Spitfires were destroyed and two pilots killed. Once again there had been trouble with gun stoppages. Eight pilots had been in a position to fire when their guns had jammed. Three pilots bailed out but were all saved. One of them was Flight Sergeant Colin Duncan of 452 Squadron.

Col Duncan's aircraft was one of the clapped out replacement Spitfires which had been sent up from the OTU in Mildura. Soon after he took off that day he realised not all was well with his machine. The engine was so worn he had difficulty keeping up with the formation even though he was running the aircraft at nearly full throttle. Now he was to experience the nightmare of every Spitfire pilot, of being trapped in the cockpit of a burning aircraft without being able to open the hood.

Looking along the long nose of the Spitfire he could see white vapour coming from one bank of exhausts. This could only mean one thing—the engine was leaking coolant and the temperature gauge was going off the clock. A haze of blue smoke filled the cockpit, and it was only a matter of time before the engine seized. Despite this, Col pressed home his attack on a Betty bomber.

Firing both his cannon and machine guns he moved his aiming point along the length of the Betty's fuselage, hoping to hit the rear gunner. But by this time it was uncomfortably hot in the cockpit, and Col decided to bail out.

He pressed the air-sea rescue button D on his radio and transmitted: 'Mayday, Mayday, Mayday. Duncan calling, bailing out.'

To do this, he had to pull the solid black rubber ball to jettison the canopy, but as he tugged at it it broke away in his hand. So much for his new aircraft! There were sheets of flame and black smoke from the engine, then it blew up. Suddenly a tongue of fire came up from under the rudder bar. Duncan suddenly remembered that the tanks were half-full, and only the firewall was between him and the main tank!

He pulled the lever to raise the seat and then found he could strike at the canopy with his elbows. Suddenly he succeeded in knocking it out a couple of inches on his left side. The 300 mile a hour slipstream whipped the canopy away, but this also had the effect of supplying oxygen to the fire and the cockpit filled with flames.

Duncan wrenched himself out of the cockpit and launched himself into the freezing air. He was still at 24 000 feet, and decided to do a delayed drop, not only to get into more breathable air but also to get out of the combat area. Zeros had been known to shoot at pilots on parachutes.

He made a heavy landing into a gum tree and found his feet dangling a couple of feet from the ground. Duncan was badly burned about the face, arms and legs and spent a miserable four days before being rescued by a search party.

Clive excelled at air fighting, so his last kill was something of an anti-climax. His quarry was not a Zero, but a fast reconnaissance aircraft, the Mitsubishi Dinah. The Dinah's job was to take intelligence photographs at altitude and it was not designed for dog-fighting.

For months, the Dinahs had been a constant source of irritation and there was now evidence that in addition to their photographic missions they had been dropping strips of metal foil to produce false images on the radar screens. The technique known in the European theatre as 'window' had first been used by British bombers to confuse German radar. Now it seemed that the Japanese had adopted it.

Clive and his number two, Flight Sergeant Paddy Padula, were scrambled at 3.30 in the afternoon and told to climb to 30 000 feet over Point Blaze. The Dinah was already under fire from the anti-aircraft guns, and Clive could clearly see the shell bursts. Looking about two miles ahead of them, he saw the Dinah flying straight and level, 4000 feet below him and 20 miles out to sea. Clive put the nose of his aircraft down and zoomed down behind him, going so fast he almost overshot his target. Clive was sure he had been seen, but the Dinah made no attempt to take evasive action, so at 50 yards he opened fire with all his guns. Infuriatingly, his starboard Hispano cannon jammed after only a few rounds but, even so, Clive saw that his shells had struck the aircraft in the fuselage, the starboard engine and the tail. It caught fire immediately and pieces of metal flew back, rattling along the sides of the Spitfire.

Now it was Padula's turn, and Clive pulled away while he made his attack. By now it was obvious that the aircraft was doomed. The Dinah was on fire in three places and trailing white smoke. Lower down now Clive pulled in behind the Mitsubishi and made a rear quarter attack from 200 yards for what he diffidently described as practice purposes.

The Spitfire was flat out. Clive glanced at the air speed indicator and saw that he was doing 360 miles an hour in the dive. He made one more attack then the Dinah staggered and began losing height. The pilot made a last effort to level out but it was obvious the aircraft was dying. It hit the water in a cloud of spray and Clive recorded the moment with his gun camera.

Clive rarely came face to face with the enemy but on this occasion he saw three bodies in the water. Two of them had parachutes attached which had partly opened. The third was a large man in a black flying suit who was spreadeagled on his back in the water face upwards.

He appeared to be still alive. Clive flew low over the water then called Fighter Control giving a fix on his position so that the bodies could be picked up. Only after the war were two of the crew identified. They were Sergeant Pilots Tomihiko Tanaka and Kinji Kawahara of the 202nd Ku. The identity of the third aviator is unknown. It was 17 August 1943 and it was to be Clive's last kill in this or any other war.

In many ways it had been an object lesson in air fighting;

what Clive was constantly drumming into his pilots. Clive subscribed to the Who-Where-When system of fixed gunnery:

Who is the enemy and what is the type of his aircraft?
Where did the pilot aim his guns?
When did he fire?—and that depended entirely upon the pilot's distance from the target.

Clive wrote:

You aim at a definite spot in space that will become full of enemy aeroplane when your bullets reach there. If you fire straight at the moving target it will be a long distance away by the time the bullet gets to the spot where you aimed. Estimation of target speed for deflection is of first importance as all subsequent work is wasted if in error.

During their first six months of operational flying against the Japanese the three squadrons had lost 37 aircraft, although only seventeen of these had been as a result of enemy action. In comparison, they had destroyed 56 Japanese aircraft and probably accounted for twelve more. Nineteen Australian and British pilots had been killed in action.

But if one is to count all the Spitfires lost in Darwin either flying operationally or non-operationally, the figure is far higher—117 aircraft. The majority of those were not lost because of technical problems or even enemy action, but because of accidents in landing and taking off. The two bush strips at Livingstone and Strauss were not that easy to land on.

Because they were surrounded by tall eucalypts, they were prone to strong cross-winds. Sometimes pilots swung off the strip and collided with the trees, while others hit parked aircraft or ended up in the drainage ditch. One pilot collided with a truck on the runway.

Another found that his rudder had jammed to starboard on landing and his undercarriage collapsed. A water bottle was found wedged between the rudder pedal and the floor, and the pilot, Flight Sergeant Coombes, was fined £10 for negligence!

Wing Commander Dick Cresswell, who had originally flown Kittyhawks from the Livingstone strip, was ordered to Darwin in 1943 to see if he could do something about the high number of training accidents. He found the accident rate for 457 and 452 Squadrons very high. It was not so high for 54 Squadron, which was using the easier Darwin aerodrome.

> When I got up there I realised they were still doing three point landings as if they were landing on grass whereas what they were doing was landing on hard fields with tall trees all around them.

Normally a pilot reduces power on landing. Cresswell ordered them to use a throttle setting of half power on landings, and the accident rate dropped by 90 per cent.

Clive commented:

The fighter ace. Clive with his Spitfire and the German, Italian and Japanese kills painted on the side of the cockpit. (AWM OG1998)

An RAF Kittyhawk. The aircraft were sometimes modified to carry both 250 and 500 pound bombs.

The opposition: a Ju 87 Stuka (*below*) and a Messerschmitt Bf 109E. The Stuka was a relatively easy target compared to the Messerschmitt. Clive shot down five Stukas in eighteen seconds. The Messerschmitt, however, was superior in every way to the Kittyhawk.

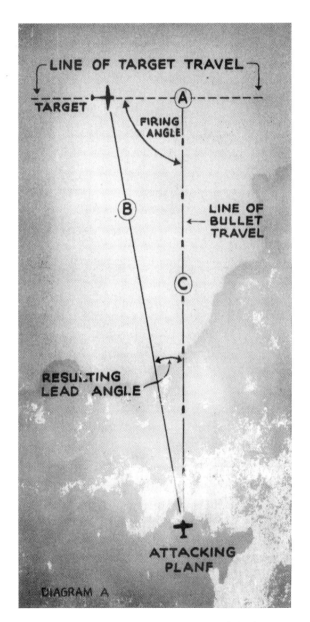

A diagram showing the technique of shadow shooting (devised by Clive) – placing the bullets ahead of the enemy aircraft so that it flew into them.

While flying with my formation at 19,000 feet approx 10 miles S of Capuzzo, glycol began to steam from my engine on the starboard side, notifying my formation leader of the situation. I cut off my throttle and turned back loosing height. At above 11.000 feet the trouble apparently cleared itself, temperature and pressure guages reading correctly so I turned West again, with a idea of overtaking the formation, flying at 12000 ft. I missed them and carried on towards Ed Adem on the chance of finding something to attack. I was observed flying West by the formation from above but not indentified as it was beleived that I had gone back. Make of my machine was recognised. After some 10 minutes in the El Adem area without seeing any a/craft in the air I proceeded further West towards Gazaia arriving in the vicinity of Bir Taieb L/G at approx 1845 hrs. I patrolled this area and at 1850 observed 2 E/A. G.50's some 4000 feet below coming from the North. Getting into position I dived and attacked one getting in a long burst with all guns. This G.50. dived and I was able to retain on it and get in a further short burst. This G.50. crashed approx 1 mile South of the road, but did not explode. The other G.50 was not in sight when I turned back to climb and at 1855 hrs flying at ground level set a compass course of 120° from a point approx 15m South of the L/G. On my course I passed through 5 camps of dispersed enemy MT, armoured cars and light tanks, each of between 40/60 vehicles. I ground strafed vehicles and personnel, injuring and killing about a dozen of the latter and saw my bullets hit several vehicles. The position of these dispersed Tanks is as follows:- Take a line approx 30 miles South of Sallum and lay back a line 300°. At intervals of 6/7 miles back along this line are the 5 points referred to altering course to 080° after passing level with sallum. Landed at Gptavela at 2000 hrs for fuel - took off and landed at own L/G at 2020hrs.

One of Clive's combat reports in which he describes the destruction of an Italian Fiat G 50. Even after the battle there was the paperwork...

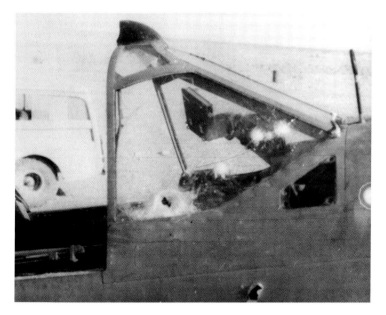

The bullet-riddled cockpit of Clive's Tomahawk. One round has penetrated the cockpit and shattered the instruments.

Clive at the controls of his damaged Tomahawk. Note the bullet hole in the canopy to the left of his head.

Two of the Luftwaffe's top scoring pilots in the desert: Hauptmann Gustav Rodel (*left*) and Lt. Werner Schroer. Schroer believed he had killed Caldwell, but in fact had only wounded him. Clive went on to destroy a Messerschmitt in his crippled aircraft.

Clive's deadly adversary: Hauptmann Hans-Joachim Marseille whose personal score was 158 aircraft. He was killed in October 1942 when he struck the tail after baling out of his aircraft.

Neville Duke, hat askew, in a celebratory mood. Beer was not always easy to come by in the desert.

Clive congratulates a Polish pilot, Sergeant Derma, after the pair shared in the destruction of an Italian Macchi C 202. Clive was held in high regard by the Poles, and was later awarded the Polish Cross of Valour.

The steely-eyed warrior. Clive was uncomfortable with the press, and hated the name 'Killer'. (AWM P02056.002)

Despite all these handicaps, the bulky air intake cowl, the metal airscrew, faulty propeller constant speed units, faulty armaments and ammunition and gun heating and engine cooling, the pilots and other musterings of No 1 Fighter Wing did a job which on the basis of enemy downed to our own losses, compared favourably with the Battle of Britain.

The Battle for Darwin had been a little skirmish compared with the Battle of Britain in which the Germans lost 1598 aircraft and the Royal Air Force 902. But Clive could take pride in the fact that he had turned a largely inexperienced group of pilots into an effective fighting force.

The last raid mounted by the Japanese against Australia was on 12 November 1943. It was the first raid in more than four months. By then the war had bypassed Darwin.

After the unfavourable publicity in the press Clive was understandably wary about talking to journalists. However, at about this time he gave an interview to John Elliott of the Australian Broadcasting Commission, who later presented a talk on radio.

Clive Caldwell, our top scoring fighter pilot, is at present commanding officer of an RAAF Spitfire formation in a Northern Operation Area I visited recently. He has shot down 27 and a half enemy planes, seven being Japs.

I suppose if Clive Caldwell happens to hear this in his tent or in his mess up north he will reach, frowning, and dowse the radio, or rise frowning and wander into the bush out of earshot—that being the way of the man.

Air Chief Marshal Sir Arthur Tedder, Deputy Supreme Commander under General Ike Eisenhower in Normandy said of Caldwell: He's a born leader and a first class shot. In the eyes of young flyers a pilot is getting on at 25, middle aged at 30, aged at 40 and after that practically ready for the crematorium, or too obstinate to lie down.

Clive Caldwell shot down his last enemy plane in September—almost a year ago. He has had little combat flying since. Recently aged 34 years he was appointed to his present command.

When the formation heard that he was coming north to take over they kept twirling their Spitfire moustaches . . .

'Whacko, now we'll see something happen,' said one.

'We'll go out on bashes every day once he's here,' said another.

'Bet he's not being sent up here for nothing,' said another.

Now to the man himself. One man reminds you of another. When I first caught sight of him he reminded me of somebody else. I was in Sydney on leave and had wandered into the crowded lobby of a Sydney hotel.

Waiting by the lifts his back towards me dressed in a dark uniform stood a big man. Unable to see his face his figure reminded me of another tall dark man—General de Gaulle.

The man by the lift had the same figure, tall as a young tree and as lean and springy hair as black as a raven, broad square shoulders, clean cut features and a certain dignity, a certain assurance. Of course I knew it couldn't be de Gaulle and then I saw his face, the colour flash of his decoration, his rank. Beside him was a slim, fair-haired woman of considerable beauty—his wife.

Perhaps at this stage it might be well to point out that, in making comparisons, whereas de Gaulle is the breath of the Free French movement, and a general, and possibly President of France, Caldwell is also a very important man. He's shot down 27 and a half assorted enemy planes over assorted theatres of war and he's done more; he's become the inspiration of not only more fighter pilots than I'd care to count before breakfast; of the hero-worshipping kids who stay awake at night hoping that a miracle will happen and they'll wake up old enough to pass the RAAF recruiting officer in the morning; but of airmen with equal and perhaps more flying hours in their logbooks.

That day in the hotel lobby all he seemed to have on his mind was the urgent need to escape the spotlight of curious eyes—for in and out of uniform Clive Caldwell is something to look at, a person easily recognised and not quickly forgotten.

I saw him many times after that; and a few days ago I saw him again standing near a Spitfire up north, gazing with appraising eyes at a lean store pig, the gift of Father McGrath of the Bathurst Island mission. The previous night, his formation had been host at a barbecue. The centrepiece was a young bullock presented by a nearby station owner, beverage being beer hoarded from time to time for the purpose from their small allotted ration.

Set up in a sandpit, the barbecue was a great success,

everyone feasting on grilled steaks washed down with near enough cool beer or lollywater, while the songsters chorused away all the Air Force songs, everyone joining in and roaring with laughter.

There was a glorious moon and, nearing midnight, they split up into two camps and then began one of those great games of RAAF rugby, Darwin version, which means roughly all in, everything goes, any number each side, tear 'em down tactics, the ball mostly forgotten, minor casualties jeered at—anything to speed up the spirit of the game, which incidentally, ends when all the players are exhausted. Its something of a moving spectacle to see possibly 50 or 60 men struggling in the moonlight, roaring with laughter struggling to get possession of a football that none can see and is anyway unnoticed at the other end of the field.

'Nights like that help to build up camaraderie, and break up the monotony of breaking our necks waiting to have a crack at the Nips,' said Clive Caldwell, still eyeing that lean store pig. It appears that two other young porkers have been promised. The three will fatten together for a future roast and barbecue.

Clive Caldwell's success secret is simple; he can fight and fly at one and the same time, but well. By fighting, I mean to deadly shoot at a diving, twisting, swerving enemy plane meanwhile protecting yourself at all times; but flying handling a plane, machine, kite or ship like a jockey racing a mount down the straight to win a Melbourne Cup, as if it were part of him. But he is more than just the king of our fighter pilots.

Fighter pilots become idols the hard way—by shooting down enemy planes. They remain idols as commanding officers, by also having that rare combination of talents which enables them to coach and inspire, command and instruct and, as well, remain first class human beings. A lesser standard is not acceptable. Another side of him is that he is a very able administrator, has everything in the formation at his finger tips, knows everything that's going on, knows everybody and soon gets to know those he doesn't. He treats them all the same from the lowly erk to his squadron leaders.

You know, he said to me, when replacements arrive I take them on strength without looking at their past records which arrive with them. I never look into them for perhaps a week sometimes two. By that time I've either flown with them or watched them work, and I have had time to form an opinion of my own as to what they have and where they miss. Only then do I read their past history.

If it isn't too good, I can't alter that, but getting to know them first it gives me a rough idea of what chance they have of making good without prejudice. Mostly I read and forget and never remember unless they do something to wake it up.

'He's not mad on flying any longer for flying's sake,' said his adjutant Flight Lieutenant Joe Jacobs of Newcastle, as a last word on Clive Caldwell.

'He's merely flying as a means of exterminating Japs.'

In September, Clive handed over command of the Spitfire Wing to Peter Jeffrey and was posted south to become chief flying instructor at the No 2 Operational Training Unit at Mildura. It was back to the circuits and bumps again.

Mildura

In the Australian spring of 1943, any odd rabbit shooter who had wandered into the dry sandhills bordering Lake Victoria near Mildura would have had a front row seat for the Spitfire in action. Hour after hour these wonderful machines flew low over the lake firing their guns. And just occasionally they flew into it.

Things had been winding down in Darwin but, when Clive returned to Mildura, he found it was buzzing with activity. Australia needed new pilots so the Victorian aerodrome was far busier than any in the Northern Territory.

There was one other advantage to being in Mildura. It meant that Jean could join him there. Instead of living on the base he moved into a hotel in town. Bruce Watson was here with his wife as well, so there was someone to socialise with. Caldwell took a shine to the fellow Sydneysider, but they always maintained a professional distance. They both had to get to the RAAF base every morning. Bruce used to take the bus but Clive offered him a lift in his car. 'It gave me a chance to get to know him. But he was always very much "Sir"; I mean there was no "Clive" for many, many years after that.'

Mildura was an ideal training base. It was warm and dry all year round, and rarely did flying have to be cancelled on account of the weather. The aerodrome reverberated to the sound of Merlin and Allison engines, and the tarmac was full of all types of aircraft, mostly trainers and fighters but bombers and transport aircraft as well. More than 1200 pilots were to pass through Mildura between 1942 and 1946.

Almost every fighter pilot who served in the South-West Pacific theatre was either trained at Mildura or did a 'refresher' course there. Most of them would never even sight the enemy, let alone fire their guns in anger. And far more would die in training accidents than be killed in action. Fifty young RAAF pilots lost their lives in training accidents in Mildura alone. Clive was keenly aware of this, and set out to improve the safety record. Flying a fighter aircraft was one thing, but it was useless unless the pilot could shoot straight.

The shadow shooting technique which Clive had pioneered in the desert had now become widely adopted. He was passionate about it and drummed it into all the trainees. In Darwin they had practised while flying over Bynoe Bay, but in Mildura they used Lake Victoria which was west of the town. Once again, Caldwell schooled his pilots to aim ahead of the shadow of the aircraft on the water. But this was an acquired skill and in was inevitable that there would be accidents.

Bruce Watson was also instructing at Mildura:

The weather down there was quiet and still, and you'd have good sunshine and you'd have a very clear shadow. But we did lose a lot of pilots because they were so keen to hit the shadow that they'd just stay there for one more burst when it was time to pull out. So quite a few dived into the lake.

You would get a student that was trailing the shadow and you'd see the bullets hit the water fifteen or 20 feet behind the shadow. So he'd have another go, he'd try to pull on a bit more G and he'd dive into the water.

When you were instructing them, you were constantly flying yourself at about 1000 feet above the water. And as soon as the pilot got down to about 500 or 600 feet, you'd start to call up and say, 'Pull out, pull out'.

Clive tutored his pilots never to fire a second burst without breaking away.

The object of shadow shooting is a self-correcting method of learning to open fire at the correct range, how to correct for deflection and the essential need to break after one burst of fire—*never* second burst without the break. Failure to break often resulted in a crashed aircraft. In a combat, it resulted in the aircraft being shot down.

There were a number of fatal accidents which came to the attention of Clive's old adversary Air Vice Marshal Jones: 'He just didn't know what the thing was all about nor bother to consult me about who had discovered and developed the system in the Middle East in 1941.'

Jones ordered that the aircraft engaged in shadow shooting must not at any point fly lower than 1000 feet. Clive retaliated by suspending gunnery practice rather than teach people to fire out of range which is what most of them did anyway.

By April 1944, it was obvious to Clive that the chances of seeing any more combat in the Pacific were remote and he requested to be posted back to the Royal Air Force in Europe. Here at least there was the prospect of flying some of the newer fighter types like the Mustang and the Thunderbolt.

George Jones refused his request and ordered him instead back to Darwin to form No 80 Fighter Wing. This was to be the central fighter wing of a group of five fighter squadrons to support Navy and Army moves to relieve Singapore later that year. The three squadrons 457, 452 and 54 were now re-equipping with the new Spitfire Mark VIIIs which were faster and had a longer range than the earlier Mark Vs. Australia was to receive 400 of the Mark VIIIs although not many of them would see any action.

Many of them were not even removed from their crates. They were placed in storage and, within just a few years, most of them would be melted down as scrap. Aluminium is a very recyclable metal and the demand for saucepans became greater than for fighter aircraft.

A good sharpshooter

In many ways Clive's life was always a gamble. He schooled his pilots never to run away from a fight, but to turn and face the enemy, to confront them head-on, guns firing. It was a lesson from his boxing days:

> A good sharpshooter makes his foe pay every time he throws a punch. Whenever a punch is blocked, slipped or weaved, it's important that you counter with multiple punches and then reinstate your jab. All of your punches should be fully extended, thus maximising your reach to the fullest.

Ferrying single-engined aircraft across water was fraught with danger, but it was an operational necessity as the RAAF moved further north from Darwin, island hopping to Merauke in West Irian, to Biak and onto Morotai Island. This was always an uneasy time for the pilots. It was uncomfortable, cold and monotonous. They sat for up to four hours behind the big throbbing Merlin, constantly checking the instruments and listening for any irregularity in the beat of the engine which might mean they had to turn back or worse still, ditch in the sea. Quite apart from the danger of long over-water flights, there was always risk associated with landing at unfamiliar or poor quality airstrips.

There had been a disaster at Merauke, when 452 Squadron lost one pilot and three aircraft in a sequence of landing accidents. Before they set off, Clive had given the pilots very precise instructions on landing at Merauke, which had an unusually long runway.

> We are landing on one of the longest strips you will ever land on. You are to land in the wheel position and, as soon as you are on the strip, you are to open the throttle, keep your tail up so you can look well ahead and you are to run to the very end of the strip before you pull the throttle off and then turn off at the last intersection. No one will land short.

The first to land was Johnny Sturn, a skilled pilot and ex-instructor. Instead of doing as he was instructed he landed short, and stopped at the first intersection in order to turn off there.

The second pilot coming in behind him, Bill Crystal, was expecting the aircraft to open up and go to the end of the strip. But the first Spitfire was blocking the runway. The second was still doing 60 miles an hour when he ran into it, his propeller slicing through the fuselage and killing Sturn.

Bruce Watson tells the story:

He opens up, but it's too late to go around again, so he goes straight into the aircraft, kills the pilot and breaks his (own) leg.

The third pilot came in to land and tried to slew his machine around the two wrecks but, unfortunately, he just clips the other aircraft and does enough damage to have to leave that particular aircraft at Merauke. The other two were written off.

The accident was due to the lack of following instructions.

The pilot had killed himself and damaged three aircraft. And one fellow with a broken leg, and the other fellow just frightened like hell.

The tragedy was that Johnny Sturn was an excellent pilot who had once successfully landed a Spitfire on a beach without doing any damage to the aircraft at all.

Now it was Bruce Watson's turn to take Spitfires up to Morotai, and he was not keen to have a repeat performance of the disaster that befell 457 Squadron. Clive, always a gambling man, bet Bruce £20 that he could not successfully fly 36 Spitfires from Darwin to Morotai without losing some. It was a grim sort of wager.

Clive said, 'You know what happened with 452?'

I said, 'Yes, that won't happen with us. We'll get 3 aircraft there.'

And he said, 'Okay. We're going to have £20.'

'Where do I get 20 quid from?'

And he said, 'Twenty quid. You're so cocky, it's 20 quid.'

A few day later Bruce shepherded his 36 Spitfires out of Darwin and out over the water towards Merauke.

The Spitfires were carrying long range belly tanks but, 20 minutes out of Darwin, one of Bruce's pilots called up to say that his tank wouldn't feed.

> And I said, 'Well, keep trying, but if it doesn't feed within the next ten minutes, let me know and I'll give you a pilot to escort you back, not right back, but to escort you back until you can see Darwin. You'll be able to see it at the height we're at.'

The belly tank still would not feed, so Watson ordered another pilot to escort the faulty Spitfire back to Darwin.

> And so I said to the other pilot, 'You've got a job to do. One is to find Darwin so as you can leave him, and the other one is to make sure you keep us in sight, so when you've left Darwin you can turn around and follow us.'

That night, Bruce joined Clive for dinner at the American mess.

Beautiful dinner we had. And he said, 'I won't make you pay for the dinner, but you owe me £20.'

I said, 'But we didn't lose an aircraft.'

He said, 'How many aircraft did you get on the ground?'

I said, '35.'

Clive said, 'The bet was 36 at Morotai, and we've only got 35 now. So you can't possibly win, can you?'

He said, 'The bet was 36 aircraft to Morotai, and you've only got 35 to Merauke.'

I had to pay.

Twenty pounds was a lot of money in those days!

I said to him, 'My wife will be without food for three weeks.'

Anyway, so I learned a lesson. I said to him, 'Thank you. I've enjoyed the dinner tonight, but it's taught me a lesson having spent the night talking to you about this. I will never have another bet with you.' And all my life, I never had another bet with Clive, because I knew he'd win every time.

A dry argument

Fighting a war was thirsty work for a drinking man like Clive Caldwell. But if alcohol had been in short supply in the desert it was even scarcer in Morotai. 'And,' queried the pilots of Number 80 Fighter Wing, 'where was Morotai exactly?' It was in the Moluccas, wherever that was. Just north of the Equator.

In the desert, it had been the sand. In Morotai, it was the mud. To those who had spent a year in the Libyan desert it might have seemed an attractive posting but Morotai was no holiday camp.

'What a dump,' thought Caldwell as he carefully taxied his Spitfire across the muddy strip. Squeezing the calliper type brakes on the control column, Clive swung the plane from side to side trying to see over the nose. The aircraft lurched through the mire. Through the almond-shaped front screen Clive could see a wasteland of discarded oil drums and bits of broken aeroplanes. 'Not so much an island paradise, more a tropical slum.'

Two parallel airstrips, Wama and Pitoe, had been carved out of the groves of tall coconut palms and when it rained they were a sea of mud. By any definition this was a hell-hole. If you were careless while you were taxiing your aeroplane, it would get stuck in the glutinous black slime. This would be followed by a lengthy and humiliating retrieval, and the subsequent ribald comments by fellow officers in what passed for a mess. Fighting the Japanese was bad enough, but the heat and humidity, the ceaseless drenching rain, the mud and insects sapped a man's will to fight.

Three days before Christmas 1944 Clive took command of Number 80 Wing, one of the wings that made up the First Tactical Air Force at Morotai. The first echelon of the wing had moved from Darwin to Noemfoor a week before.

'What a bloody awful place to spend Christmas,' thought Clive. Thank God he had sequestered away a little Christmas cheer. Under the seat in his Spitfire was a single bottle of whisky, but in the big Douglas C 47 transport which followed there was enough booze to float a battleship. There were eighteen bottles of Australian whisky, six bottles of Scotch, eighteen bottles of gin, five and a half dozen bottles of beer, and ten bottles of mixed wines, sherry and port.

It was while he was in Darwin that Clive had become alive to the commercial possibilities of selling liquor at Morotai. The airfield was shared with a number of thirsty American squadrons whose pilots would pay handsomely for hard liquor, ten times what it would cost in Australia.

Over the next two months Clive arranged for large quantities of liquor to be shipped to Morotai, some by aircraft and some by sea. Towards the end of January 1945, he went back to Darwin to arrange for the rest of the squadron's equipment to be brought to Morotai. While he was there he persuaded the crew of an American B 24 Liberator bomber to bring in another small consignment, mostly whisky, sherry and gin. There was not much room in a Spitfire to carry any more than one or two bottles. But a four-engined bomber like a Liberator was four times as big as a Spitfire and had lots of nooks and crannies where liquor could be hidden.

The booze run continued into the new year. In March, an Australian navy corvette docked at Morotai with 50 bottles, mostly whisky, gin and rum. Clive was paying fourteen shillings for a bottle of Scotch. In Morotai he could get ten pounds for it.

•

Clive's antipathy towards Air Vice Marshal George Jones was well known. The latest confrontation had been over the proposed landings at Tarakan but before that there had been the rows over the Spitfire's armament, Clive's criticism of the Boomerang and the problems with locally made ammunition.

20:00 hours Tactical Air Force HQ Morotai. A meeting to discuss 'Oboe One', the proposed landings at Tarakan in Borneo.

The purpose: to deny the Japanese the precious oil supplies and to secure the airstrip for further operations.

Those present: Air Vice Marshal George Jones, Air Commodore Harry Cobby, Group Captains Gibson and Simms and Group Captain Clive Caldwell.

CALDWELL: 'Tarakan? With respect you have to be joking, Sir. It would be like the Dieppe raid.'

(The Dieppe raid in France in August 1942 had cost 900 lives, mostly Canadians)

JONES: 'What do you mean, Caldwell?'

CALDWELL: 'What I mean, Sir, is that to justify the trust of those I lead in the air, it is essential I have confidence in what is planned and its reasonable prospect of success.'

JONES: 'Your task is to be a tactical leader. There are strategic considerations involved which do not concern you.'

CALDWELL: 'Sir, I have flown over Tarakan and in my view a landing is out of the question. I must impress upon you the futility of it. I estimate we could lose 1000 men and as many wounded, and it will take more than three weeks before the island could be used as a stepping stone to Balikpapan.'

JONES: 'You do realise, Caldwell, that it is essential for us to occupy Tarakan to deny the Japanese the oil?'

CALDWELL: 'Sir, that is bloody nonsense. Surely it has reached even Melbourne by now that the oil from Tarakan has been doused for at least the last seven weeks? The Japanese have no oil.'

COBBY: 'Caldwell, strategic planning is not your business.'

CALDWELL: 'Sir, with respect, there are problems of landing and securing Tarakan and those of proper air cover.'

JONES: 'You are to mount the operation as ordered.'

CALDWELL: 'Sir, I wish to lodge a strong protest, and I want it clearly noted and confirmed on the record.'

JONES: 'You will comply with this order!'

CALDWELL: 'Sir, if you mount this operation in the light

of all I have pointed out then you ought to be looked at as of diminished responsibility.'

Caldwell shot a glance at Jones's personal assistant Wing Commander Lindeman and continued: 'And I wish that placed on the record.'

Caldwell stormed from the room. Jones was speechless with rage. To be publicly humiliated in front of fellow officers was the last straw. Caldwell must go. Clive knew that he would now face some sort of disciplinary action. Since a posting to the Royal Air Force had been denied the only avenue open to him was to leave the service. His fall from grace was assured, his demotion inevitable. On 1 May 1945 the invasion of Tarakan went ahead as planned without Clive Caldwell.

As Clive had prophesied, the landing was a disaster although the loss of life was nowhere near as high as he had predicted. The invasion was supposed to last a week; in fact it dragged on for two months and cost 240 Australian lives. The 4000 Japanese were well prepared in concrete bunkers and tunnels, and had left behind many booby traps. They fought aggressively until the end when the survivors melted away into the interior.

The remaining Japanese were hunted by patrols, and many were captured attempting to leave by improvised rafts. The purpose of the operation had been to secure the airstrip, which could then be used as a stepping stone to continue operations into Java. But the airfield was so badly damaged during Allied air raids that it was not ready to receive aircraft until the end of June by which time all further operations had been cancelled.

The aim was also to deny the Japanese the oil reserves on the island, but these had been heavily bombed in December

1944 and only about twelve per cent of the island's storage capacity remained. Tarakan proved to be a stepping stone to nowhere. And this was as true for Caldwell's career as for the military operation on Tarakan . . .

It was inevitable that Jones would try to cut him down to size. What followed were two events that were to rock the foundations of the Royal Australian Air Force and to tarnish Clive's reputation—Clive's court martial and a commission of enquiry. Generally the RAAF had turned a blind eye to officers carrying in to their base one or two bottles of liquor for their own personal consumption or to give to their friends.

On 1 August 1944, new orders specifically relating to the Pacific area had been circulated to all RAAF bases. These orders gave the RAAF Canteen Services Unit exclusive control of the order, distribution, quantity restriction, pricing and all other matters to do with alcoholic liquor in the Pacific Areas outside mainland Australia. (See paragraph 7 of Air Board Orders 'N' 548 of 1944.)

This meant was that the unit messes, unit canteens or other semi-official institutions were not allowed to buy liquor from any source other than the Canteen Services Unit. RAAF members could only buy from their mess or canteen. No member, unless it was part of their duty, could sell alcoholic liquor and no aircraft, vessel or ship owned by or on loan to the RAAF could be used to carry alcoholic liquor to any place in the Pacific area outside mainland Australia, except for the Canteen Services Unit.

At the time of the issue of the orders, pilots and others had become accustomed to purchasing supplies, usually when in

Darwin, and tucking a bottle or two away in their aircraft before returning to the base in the Pacific area outside the mainland of Australia. As the war progressed and the air force hopped from island to island Canteen Services were slow to catch up and usually did not have any liquor in stock!

These orders became notorious because they claimed to be not widely known and, where known, were ignored or at the very least, difficult to police. The 'N' orders were also at the centre of the trouble which dogged Clive Caldwell throughout 1945 and beyond.

Even after August 1944, a blind eye might still have been turned to personnel bringing in liquor, especially as in these areas the RAAF canteen was often out of supplies. Carrying in a bottle or two was one thing. Clive, however was charged with *trading* in it.

On 10 April 1945, Clive was notified that certain charges had been preferred against him, that he was under open arrest and that he was to parade before the officer temporarily commanding Headquarters 1st Tactical Air Force Squadron Leader Grey-Smith. There were five charges of 'Conduct to the Prejudice of Good Order and Air Force Discipline,' each relating to an incident of alleged selling of alcoholic liquor 'contrary to paragraph 7 of ABO "N" 548 of 1944'.

To his intense humiliation, Clive was placed under arrest and suspended from his appointment as Commanding Officer of 80 Wing and attached to the No 3 Reserve Personnel Pool. The court martial was set for 21 April but, because of the war, many of the witnesses were needed elsewhere so it was dissolved.

Clive was released from arrest but was told that he could be re-arrested at any time. In fact the court martial would not be reconvened until January 1946, five months after the war had ended.

Clive had had enough and tried to resign his commission. He wrote to Cobby:

> This operational tour, in its absence of true operations, has been a big disappointment to me and I am not reassured by the prospects of appointments available to me at home. Therefore if it is a fact that this incident is the opportunity to make an example of me, I respectfully request that my commission be terminated.

The news of Clive Caldwell's arrest spread like wildfire among fellow officers, already disenchanted with the way in which Australian forces had been marginalised by the Americans. Eleven days after Clive had been charged with the liquor offences, the unthinkable happened. Seven other senior officers in the Royal Australian Air Force followed suit and resigned their commissions. All of them believed that the liquor trading was trivial. Everybody was doing it. The wider issue was the conduct of the war.

Three pilots—Group Captain Wilf Arthur, Wing Commander John Waddy and Wing Commander Bobby Gibbes—were highly decorated fighter aces. The other four, Wing Commander Ranger and Squadron Leaders Grace, Vanderfield and Harpham were experienced fliers.

The eight pilots had first met together in Squadron Leader

Harpham's quarters. All agreed that the operations they were carrying out were useless and that there must be some dishonest or improper purpose behind them. They talked for hours trying to work out a plan of action. Caldwell, who was always impatient, wanted an immediate decision but the meeting broke up without a conclusion having been reached.

On 19 April they met again and decided to resign simultaneously hoping that this drastic action would focus the powerful force of public opinion on affairs at Morotai. They all typed identical letters using the same typewriter.

As written later in the report of a Commission of Enquiry, they wanted:

> . . . leaders of integrity who would resist outside pressure and an honest, economical prosecution of the war. Their aim was an independent investigation by an impartial competent authority, and they were prepared to go to extreme lengths to secure it. They acted from the highest motives of patriotism. All of them knew well that they were probably sacrificing all hope of permanent careers in the Air Force.

The mutiny had been orchestrated in part by Wilf Arthur, a popular and experienced pilot, who had arrived in Noemfoor in December as commander of 81 Wing. He had quickly come to the conclusion that the targets being attacked were not worthwhile and that the RAAF was wasting time, risking expensive aircraft, endangering people's lives and squandering bombs and ammunition.

He drew up a balance sheet to demonstrate the futility of

the operations. Over a three month period it attempted to assess the value—in pilots killed, aircraft destroyed and petrol, bombs and ammunition expended—of the damage inflicted on the enemy. Arthur's balance sheet concluded that the only things of value to the enemy which had been destroyed were motor transport and barges and that the wing had lost eleven men and fifteen aircraft to destroy twelve barges and six motor transports.

It showed that in October and November 1944, the aircraft of 81 Wing had flown nearly 2000 hours and taken part in 1125 sorties, consumed 87 450 gallons of fuel, dropped 428 150 pounds of bombs and expended nearly half a million rounds of ammunition. Arthur had shown his balance sheet to Cobby, who appreciated it, but concluded that the losses were not great in terms of the numbers of sorties flown. He had missed the point Arthur and others were trying to make— the wasteful use of effort and expertise for trivial purposes.

To Arthur, the balance sheet very clearly proved that men were being killed and valuable equipment lost, for no very good purpose. These were young fit men, superbly trained and equipped, eager to come to grips with the enemy and play a full part in the defeat of the Japanese. But instead of operating in the forward areas with the Americans they found themselves in stagnant backwaters flying long boring patrols for little or no result. They blamed their superior officers in the Air Board. But in fact it was not their fault. The First Tactical Air Force was receiving its orders from the United States 13th Air Force.

When the pilots tendered their resignations Bill Bostock wrote a cable to Jones, which he showed Cobby before sending.

In Melbourne in April 1945, George Jones received word from Morotai that eight of his most experienced fighter pilots had attempted to resign and their superior officers had obviously lost all credibility to command. 'What the bloody hell is going on?' he said.

A desperate signal came from Bill Bostock:

Morale throughout 1st Tactical Air Force is at a dangerous low level . . . demeanour of all officers during my interview with them was respectful, but bitter and unrelenting. From general observations, I am convinced that the attitude of the officers who have asked to resign is a reliable index to the widespread dissatisfaction which pervades the whole Tactical Air Force.

Bostock and Harry Cobby interviewed seven of the eight officers and demanded they state the reasons for their actions but they all refused. They did however agree to drop the word 'forthwith' from their applications and substitute the words 'on completion of impending operations' to avoid any possible accusation that they wanted to resign rather than take part in the Tarakan operations.

All of the officers respected Cobby but were less enamoured of Group Captains Gibson and Simms. Bostock would probably have been happier to handle the matter himself but now Jones would have to be involved. Relations between Bostock and Jones had never been good, and those under their command were never sure as to who was actually running the Air Force. Theoretically, Jones was in charge of

Air Force operations in Australia and Bostock in the islands. Bostock requested that Air Commodore Cobby and Group Captains Gibson and Simms should immediately be relieved of their appointments. This was an unfortunate blow to Harry Cobby, who had spent his whole life in the RAAF and had been a famous fighter ace in World War I.

Cobby was liked and respected, but he was past his prime and considered by Jones to be too old for the job. He had isolated himself from those under his command by living in separate quarters with his two senior staff officers, Group Captains Gibson and Simms. Jones sacked Cobby, Gibson and Simms on the spot and arranged to interview the seven officers. Because of his pending court martial, Caldwell was to be dealt with separately.

The atmosphere was tense and Wilf Arthur spoke coldly and deliberately:

'You are the Chief of the Air Staff,' he said, 'Why don't you go and see MacArthur and thump the table and demand that we be taken to the Philippines?'

Jones replied: 'Curtin has done his utmost in that direction. If he tried and failed how do you think that I could succeed?'

It was well established that MacArthur wanted only American forces to return in triumph to the Philippines, with assistance from no other force. This precluded the involvement of the Australians and the New Zealanders who were left behind to do the mopping up.

While Jones was still on the island, General Kenney arrived

from the Philippines and also demanded to see the seven fliers. As diplomatically as he could, Jones pointed out to the American that it was none of his business and that these matters were purely disciplinary ones outside his jurisdiction. He insisted being present during the interview.

Kenney harangued the pilots for hours and implored them not to hand in their badges, but the seven officers were quite adamant about their resignations, and nothing that Kenney could say would placate them. By the time the interview finished, Kenney was seething with anger.

He turned on Jones, 'You had to stay and listen to everything I had to say. Evidently you don't trust me!'

'This was a disciplinary matter. So it was wholly my concern,' said Jones.

Kenney was now so angry that Jones fully expected him to physically attack him.

> I was quite ready for him. I told him I'm concerned that our forces should cooperate fully to win this war.
>
> The remark seemed to cool him down. He agreed that it was indeed vital for Americans and Australians to cooperate, so we shook hands and parted on reasonably amicable terms.

Questions were now being asked in Canberra. Who exactly was running the Royal Australian Air Force?

'Bloody amateurs down south too far from the sound of gunfire,' growled Caldwell.

Why were the pilots so disenchanted with their task?

After all, the RAAF had never been in better shape; it had 40 operational squadrons anxious to earn their keep. But the Americans, and in particular their commander, General Douglas MacArthur, had no intention of sharing the final fruits of victory with their Australian allies.

Japanese air raids had ceased apart from the occasional reconnaissance flight so the Spitfire's duties consisted largely of mopping up operations attacking pockets of Japanese resistance on the ground—enemy ships, fuel dumps, barges, gun positions. It was a poor substitute for aerial combat.

The pilots chafed at doing this dangerous work and the losses were high. The Spitfire was not an ideal aircraft for ground attack, and a stray round in the engine could prove disastrous. They knew that if they were shot down over enemy territory they could expect no mercy from the Japanese. The enemy was low on food, fuel and ammunition, and their supply lines had been cut; it seemed pointless to risk the lives of pilots on an enemy that no longer presented any real threat.

Clive Caldwell had found that the spirits of the pilots had risen when they had first moved to Morotai from Darwin, because they hoped they would be involved in air fighting. In fact there was little prospect of meeting the enemy in the air. Some of them were brassed off at the lack of activity and resented newspaper reports which exaggerated, criticised or glamourised what they were doing.

Clive was in his element in the air, and hated the inactivity on the ground. There were no more fighters but attacking something was better than doing nothing.

However if there was no danger in the air it would be easy

to be complacent about the danger on the ground. Especially anti-aircraft guns hidden in the trees. Clive's technique was to flush them out.

He would fly fairly slowly along the hills to try to provoke the guns to fire. Bruce Watson flew as Caldwell's number two and gives some insight as to the dangerous nature of the missions:

The Japanese were still entrenched only 50 miles away on the islands surrounding Morotai. Nobody was too worried about them. They couldn't do any harm; no shipping could get to them so they couldn't be re-supplied very easily and in time they were literally going to die out. But it wasn't worth sending troops over to capture them.

Clive liked to have a purpose and his purpose was to try to destroy some of these mountain gunners.

He used to waffle along in front of the mountains, and he would be watching for the smoke from the guns. The minute that happened, he'd do something rather drastic with his aircraft and then it'd be your turn to waffle past, and he'd watch for the gun and then, when you saw the gun fire, you'd go in and try to hit it with cannon shells.

The Japanese were using their 75 millimetre anti-aircraft gun which could make a very nasty hole in an aeroplane.

Often the Spitfires would fly around for hours without finding anything to shoot at. One day Clive and Bruce caught a Japanese staff car in the open:

We took great delight in shooting it up. We worked on the theory there wouldn't be any normal people working there like a station manager or a property owner: it would obviously have been Japanese. You might find a Japanese truck, and with a little bit of luck you might find a camp site. Those were the silly sort of targets you were looking for.

They often returned our fire.

But you only need a bullet in the radiator or the engine and you were in real trouble.

Clive later wrote:

The attacks on bypassed Japanese forces in and around the Halmaher has brought these enemy forces quite unnecessarily into action with our free forces, instead of being left to wither on the vine where they could do no harm.

Clive felt that shooting up ground targets was better than nothing. He would say to Watson: 'Well, at least we know they're there. We've stirred them up somewhat.'

Edward Sly also flew with Clive on ground attack missions. Clive told Ted: 'I'll show you what this war's all about.'

Clive would lead the attack himself as they dived onto targets. Clive's aircraft would normally have the element of surprise but, by the time the second aircraft was over the target, the anti-aircraft gunners had drawn a bead on it.

Attacking a Japanese anti-aircraft position on an island 200 miles south of Morotai, Ted made one strafing run and unwisely returned for a second. The Japanese gunners had deserted the gun but left it firing on automatic. It blew a hole in the wing, but Ted flew safely back to base. Ted knew of two fighter pilots who had been beheaded by the Japanese. As he said:

> One of our greatest fears when operating over the Pacific was to be captured by the Japanese. We sometimes passed over large groups of them, but the thought of capture was worse than landing in shark-infested waters.

If the war had bypassed Morotai it was still raging 800 miles away in the Philippines. Manila had fallen the previous month, and 400 000 Japanese had died in the fighting. Clive had wanted to be where the action was, and pestered Kenney about taking Spitfires to the Philippines. Caldwell was Kenney's good friend but General Douglas MacArthur had his own ideas. When he returned to the Philippines it was to be exclusively an American victory.

On 24 March, however, Clive Caldwell was also to return to the Philippines. When the Americans had taken Clark Field they had captured a huge number of new Japanese aircraft and were keen to see how well they performed when flown against Allied types like the Spitfire. Caldwell agreed to take up four Spitfires escorted by two Mosquitos.

The episode was almost to cost him his life.

Running on empty

It was the worst tropical storm Bruce Watson had ever seen. The top of the black and grey cloud was very high—maybe 30 000 feet. The base seemed to be resting on the ocean which was an angry mass of green water flecked with foam. He pressed his radio transmit button: 'Red Leader, I don't want to go through that.'

Clive Caldwell radioed back: 'No, we won't go through it. We'll go over the top of it.'

Four Spitfires and two Mosquitos were over the Sulu Sea, two hours out from Morotai, heading for Clark Field in the Philippines. There had been no problems on the flight so far, but the weather was getting worse, and this was a long journey over water in a single-engined aircraft.

The Spitfires were carrying two 90 gallon long range tanks but, even then, it was touch and go whether they would make it or not.

Said Bruce:

We'd been assured that if we were at any stage short of fuel in the last 200-300 miles, there were plenty of airfields that we could drop into short of Manila. But we probably could have made it in one hop with a little bit of luck.

The Mosquitos meanwhile, had plenty of fuel and, could fly twice as far as the Spitfires. Caldwell and Watson were formatting on the Mosquitos but the visibility was so bad they occasionally disappeared in the murk. Clive called the Mosquitos and told them to climb. The word came back; they can't go higher—the oxygen tanks on the aircraft *had not been filled!*

The two Mosquitos had been serviced prior to take-off but neither of them had requested oxygen, so they were unable to go up to any height.

The best way of avoiding the storm was by going towards the east, but this took the four aircraft away from the direct route to Manila. Meanwhile the weather was getting worse; lightning crashed on the horizon and the little Spitfires were being thrown around by strong wind gusts.

The four aircraft continued on their new flight path for an hour when Caldwell and Watson realised that the top of the storm was even higher than they had originally thought, maybe 35 000 feet. Bruce radioed Caldwell again:

Red Leader, I think we ought to have a check with the Mosquitos to what our position is. We're further away from the coast the more we go around the storm.

Clive agreed and called up the Mosquitos: 'Give us a check where you think our position is. Obviously over the sea, but in relation to the Philippine coastline.'

The word came back from the Mosquitos: 'We haven't been navigating; we wouldn't know.'

'Christ Almighty,' said Caldwell. The radio waves were suddenly full of blue language.

Clive pressed his transmit button and radioed Watson: 'Well, what do we do? What're your thoughts?'

The six aircraft were now hopelessly lost and a long way from land. It was a case of the blind leading the blind. Clive was furious that the Mosquitos had not been navigating. After a brief discussion with Watson, they agreed to steer a course 290 degrees and the other two aircraft would steer 270; hopefully one or the other would strike land.

Clive and Bruce conferred and decided they would not take their aircraft over the top of the cloud alone. The only other option was to go underneath it, which would bring them down to wave-top height.

Bruce was terrified:

I've been in some frightening storms before, but when we finally got to the bottom of the storm, we were literally no more than feet above the ocean.

And the waves were breaking in such a way that at one stage I called up one of the Mosquitos and said to Paddy Dempster the pilot, 'Remember this, we don't want to surf. We've got to keep above those waves.'

It was absolutely pouring. But we battled on and I didn't know whether we were going to literally hit a wave—the waves seemed to be coming up—or whether we'd disappear and lose the Mosquitos in the storm.

They had been following the lights on the Mosquitos, but it was so dark now they couldn't see them, so the Spitfires turned their navigation lights on. Bruce's eyes strained in the blackness, hoping to catch a glimpse of Kel Barclay's Spitfire. But the weather was so bad he couldn't see it. There was a real risk that the aircraft would collide in the murk.

I couldn't see Kel Barclay so I called up and said, 'Kel, are you okay?'

And he came back and said, 'Yes, why do you ask?'

And I said, 'Well, I just looked or glanced across, and I couldn't see you at all in the blackness.'

He said, 'Well, I haven't even looked across to see if you're still there, but I'm okay.'

Watson and Barclay flew on for another 40 minutes. The Spitfires were dangerously low on fuel and they were too busy concentrating on flying to make anything but the briefest radio communication:

We didn't hear anything from the others, except occasionally they would make a bit of a check and say much the same—'Everything running all right?' And not much more.

With sudden relief Bruce realised he was over land:

> There appeared some cliffs and some trees and I realised
> that we'd actually hit the coast and I called out to Kel, 'Go
> under me. Go under me and I'll go up.' So I went up and
> Kel Barclay slid across under me to the other side of me
> and we all turned fairly violently because we'd actually hit
> the Philippine coastline.

The storm hadn't abated but at least they were over land.
Clive however was still lost over the sea, vainly following the
other Mosquito.

Bruce radioed Clive:

> We've hit the coastline, and we're now flying almost north,
> still in bad weather, but it looks like it might be improving
> a little. Where are you?
>
> Clive said, 'We're flying north up the coastline. We're
> obviously following you, but we're still in very bad weather
> conditions.'
>
> And then he said, 'I'm just going to give Len some
> instructions.' And then we heard him say, 'Len, if you have
> to bail out, I want you to give me 30 seconds' to one
> minute's warning, because I'll bail out with you, but I'm
> taking that Mosquito down first. I will shoot that Mosquito
> down for its stupidity and then we'll both bail out.'

Clive Caldwell was furious and there is no doubt in Bruce's
mind that he would have done what he said.

Anyway, so, about ten minutes later, we heard him call again. He said, 'Len, how's your fuel supply?'

And Len said, 'It's bloody low, but I'm still flying.'

A few minutes later Clive Caldwell again repeated his threat to shoot down the Mosquito.

'You know what I want,' said Clive.

'I want two minutes' or a minute's warning. If necessary, give me five seconds' warning, but give me enough warning. I've got my guns turned on and I'm just ready to shoot. But we're not going into the sea without that Mosquito.'

By this time Len Reed had used up most of the fuel in his 90 gallon tank and had switched back to the main tank. Bruce Watson, meanwhile, had spotted some American cruisers below, and suggested to Clive that if they had to ditch there was a good chance of being picked up. He unsuccessfully tried to contact them by radio.

A short time later in the distance he saw the faint outline of two aircraft flying over the sand. They were American Dakota transport aircraft. They had made it! There must be an airfield nearby—not Clark Field, but another wartime strip.

Bruce Watson was certain that Kel Barclay's aircraft was even lower on fuel than his and out of consideration for the less experienced pilot told him to land first. This was not the strip they had been looking for but this was an emergency and both aircraft were running on empty. It was a case of any airport in a storm: 'You land first. I know I've got another few minutes' fuel. I'll follow you in.'

The strip they landed at, however, could not by any definition be described as an airport. It was called Dulag, a rough satellite landing ground fringed with palm trees and surrounded by pools of stagnant water. There were no buildings, just a dispersal area where other American aircraft were parked. But mercifully there was a fuel tanker.

Kel Barclay's Spitfire landed first and Bruce followed him in. The two Spitfires managed to make it just before the first of the Mosquitos landed. So far so good. Clive Caldwell and Len Reed were still out there, battling the storm, so Watson and Barclay sat on the ground listening to their radios hoping against hope that their mates were safe. Over the radio Caldwell was still threatening to shoot down one of the Mosquitos.

Bruce recalled:

Every three or four minutes we'd get this call, 'Len, you still okay? I still want that minute's notice, because that Mosquito's going in if we go in.'

At least Caldwell and Reed were still in the air. After what seemed to be an eternity Clive's voice came over the radio. 'We have found the strip. There's the strip. Thank goodness!'

The last two Spitfires flew into the circuit and lowered their undercarriages. Len Reed landed first and, after he turned off the strip, his motor cut dead. He was out of fuel.

Bruce and some of the others ran down the strip to push

him out of the way when somebody shouted, 'Look out! Look at the other one!'

> And we looked back and Clive was at about 500 feet with his motor stopped. There's his prop, absolutely stuck, standing still. And so he made a dead stick landing. And, of course, after he ran to a stop, together with the aid of many Americans we had to run down and push him out of the way.

Caldwell had been in the air for four hours and fifteen minutes by the time his motor cut. Bruce and the other pilots helped push the Spitfire off the strip onto the taxiway. Clive undid his harness and leapt from the aircraft, his face as black as thunder. As he did so, he pulled out his revolver. Bruce tried to stop him, but Clive pulled his hand away and started walking across the strip towards the second Mosquito, which had now landed and was taxiing in. 'I'm gonna use that. I'm gonna shoot that bastard. He just nearly cost us two lives and two Spitfires.'

Bruce once more tried to take the gun from the senior officer, but Clive was taller, stronger, and very determined. It became a wrestling match.

> I said, 'Sir, this is not the place. I don't really know how you feel because it didn't happen to me, but I can imagine how you would feel. At least we made it here. But we've already done a rough check and I think we had about eight gallons left when we landed, so we're really in a different position to you without any fuel, and a dead motor.'

Bruce put his hand on the revolver and said: 'This is not the time. Give me the gun.'

Finally, after a few minutes, Clive handed Watson his pistol.

How certain was Bruce that he would have used it?

I'd have to be honest, and say that I think he was determined to do what he'd said he was going to do. But I think he also might have felt from the words I used that, perhaps, he was acting in absolute anger and it might be better if he just waited a while.

Bruce Watson kept the gun for two hours, by which time Clive's anger had subsided a little. Fortunately for everyone, he did not shoot the Mosquito pilot, Alec Barrett: 'But he was still extremely angry, as I think you can imagine he would be.'

Nearly 60 years after the event, Bruce Watson is certain that Clive meant what he said.

The Americans could only give them enough fuel to get them to their intended aerodrome, inland and 30 miles south. They had flown over it during the incoming flight, but somehow missed it in the bad weather.

The aerodrome had a proper mess, food, liquor and accommodation. Bruce Watson slept very well that night but, before he fell asleep, he reflected on how lucky he was to be in a bed and not sitting on the bottom of the Sulu Sea.

Clive's entry in his log book gives no indication of the drama that surrounded the Philippines flight. It reads:

Morotai-Dulag. Bad weather heavy rain for two and half hours. Navigating aircraft lost self and No 2 homed Dulag under three gallons petrol <u>out</u> all tanks.

If the Spitfire squadrons had been expressly forbidden to take part in any combat in the Philippines why did they fly there anyway? The intention was that the Spitfires and Mosquitos would be tested in mock attacks on captured Japanese aircraft.

But this was just a ploy. Clive hoped that as soon as the aircraft were based in Manila they could take part in operations alongside the Americans. When the Spitfires arrived in Manila the Australians found the airfield full of captured Japanese aircraft but they had either been damaged or were not flyable. There was nothing for the Spitfires to fly against.

Unfortunately, the word got back to Melbourne and, when George Jones found out that there was to be no test flying, he very smartly put an embargo on the Spitfire pilots taking part in any other operations.

Bruce Watson had been left in charge in Manila, while Clive flew back to Morotai to attend his court martial.

I received some very strong cables from George Jones, expressly forbidding any unauthorised operations alongside the Americans, clearly pointing out what my authorities were, and what would happen to any of the fellows if any of them were lost in unauthorised operations.

We were sitting with four of the greatest fighters in the world and the Americans just were begging us to come out, come on some of their raids with them and we had to sit there and say, 'I'm sorry, but we're not allowed'.

But we hung on in the hopes that something would happen and also, of course, this was part of Clive's plan to get Spitfires into Manila.

The pilots consoled themselves by putting on flying displays for the Americans. The Americans were impressed: 'Why the hell can't you come and work with us?'

When Clive was recalled to Australia to attend his court martial, other pilots flew Clive's personalised Spitfire CR-C, including Flight Lieutenant Edward Sly. The aircraft was fitted with an 87 gallon long-range tank in preparation for the return flight back to Morotai, and Ted took it on a test flight to see that there was a continuous fuel flow when switching from tank to tank.

Ted climbed to to 1200 feet and switched to the long range tank. The motor cut dead. He turned back to Clark Field, preparing to do a dead stick landing, and just had enough air speed to clear an outdoor movie screen.

The aircraft made a heavy landing and broke in two. Ted leapt out of the aircraft and onto the wing, but forgot to disconnect the plug connecting the headset with the radio. The lead dragged him back into the aircraft. Fortunately for Ted, there was no fire. 'Clive never let me forget that I crashed his aircraft at Clark Field in the Philippines,' said Ted.

If there was one consolation about the Spitfire's deployment to Manila it was the fact that Bruce Watson finally got his hands on an aircraft he had flown against in combat so many times—the Zero. It was a captured example, with no armament and no armour plating, and Bruce found it a delight to fly. He decided to fly it back to Morotai, this time avoiding a long direct flight over water by making a refueling stop at Zamboanga.

A number of other Australian pilots flew the machine at Morotai but did not treat it with the same degree of care. The aeroplane developed a serious oil leak and was in the process of being repaired when word came through that the squadrons were leaving for Labuan in Borneo. Bruce thinks that the Zero was probably scrapped by the Americans and pushed off the strip with a grader.

Had Clive paid for the aircraft in whisky? In handwritten notes from 1989 he writes:

Two bottles of my whisky to the C/O U.S. Technical Intelligence got us a fully serviceable Zero with Watson back to Morotai—very valuable indeed.

It appears that Clive *was* keen to acquire Japanese aircraft during his brief time in the Philippines. The Barry Commission was told that on 15 March 1945 he took a case of mixed liquor to Manila in a Douglas C 47 transport.

. . . which he was visiting for the purposes of test flying of interception aircraft Allied and enemy in collaboration with the Americans. The purpose was to acquire certain captured Japanese aircraft. The trip proved abortive and none of the liquor was used.

On the return journey a quantity of liquor was lost (probably wine) because the corks blew out at altitude!

Clive's last operation with the RAAF was on 25 March 1945. His logbook records a patrol in the Manila area, Bataan and Corregidor. All told he had flown on 496 operational sorties in the Middle East, Europe and in the Pacific, and had flown 1116 hours.

The Barry Commission

At the end of a distinguished flying career Clive Caldwell was to be put on trial. First he had to give evidence at a commission of enquiry, then later he was to face a court martial.

As anticipated, the press had given plenty of publicity to both the pilots' attempts to resign their commissions and the court martial of one of the most prominent fighter pilots of the war years. Clive had been one of the pin-up boys, used extensively by RAAF Public Relations to promote the Air Force and was now in disgrace or at least in the forefront of overdue revelations of the RAAF administration's ineptitude.

The assumed conflict between Clive and his superior, Cobby, was also extensively discussed. Clive liked Cobby but did not let this stop him from pursuing what he perceived to be a lack of sound leadership from the highest ranks.

This public speculation could not continue, and on 11 May 1945 Air Minister Drakeford commissioned a comprehensive enquiry into all aspects of the situation.

The enquiry was to examine which members of 1st Tactical Air Force dealt in alcoholic liquor in any way—brought it in, disposed of, sold, or exchanged it. It would also examine, if this was so, if the Air Officer Commanding of the First Tactical Air Force was aware of and took appropriate steps against such actions. The enquiry extended to whether Air Commodore Bladin or Air Commodore De La Rue dealt in alcoholic liquor and whether any of Clive Caldwell's allegations about senior officers were correct. It would also cover the matter of RAAF aircraft being used in dealing with alcoholic liquor and, if shown to be so, if the Air Officer Commanding of the First Tactical Air Force was aware of this and took steps to stop such use of aircraft. The commission was also able to examine any other matters which they found were related to any of the stated issues.

The commission of enquiry began on 16 May, heard by the distinguished Kings' Counsel, John V. Barry. It was to examine two tightly linked issues—the operational leadership of the First Tactical Air Force and liquor trading among its officers. Unfortunately for Caldwell, it was the liquor trading that attracted most of the publicity.

More serious—and what the officers in handing in their resignations had hoped to have addressed—was the lack of leadership and the unresolved bickering between George Jones and William Bostock, and the fact that the RAAF's efficiency and morale was poor compared with that of the Army and Navy. The squabbles among the top brass, as one wag remarked, were enough to drive anyone to drink!

The inquiry was to drag on for four months, sitting first

in Melbourne then, because the 107 witnesses to be examined on oath were so scattered, it moved to Townsville, Morotai, Madang, Bougainville and Tadji, finally resuming in Melbourne on 28 June. Despite there being considerable interest shown by the press, the hearing was held in private because of security issues concerning information about operational units. The full report was not published but a summary statement was issued on 14 September 1945.

A hand lifted the tent flap to reveal a dozen Americans standing in line. They all needed a drink. There were 70 000 of them and they had no liquor at all on Noemfoor Island; but they did have money. At Noemfoor, the ship bringing three months supply of liquor for the Australians had been swinging at anchor offshore for some weeks. When the boxes of beer and spirits were finally unloaded from the ship, they were under heavy guard.

According to Harry Cobby the precautions taken were so effective that the loss from thefts and breakage was about three per cent which was 'remarkably small in the circumstances'. The landing of this liquor, reported Cobby, 'was to give rise to problems of an unprecedented kind'.

Officers were allowed to drink spirits, the men got two bottles of beer a week worth about 1 shilling 3 pence a bottle. The Americans, however, were prepared to pay 25 shillings for a bottle of beer or barter it for five cartons of cigarettes. Nice work if you can get it. If you were entitled to two bottles of beer a week, but could do without it you could make yourself £10 —2500 per cent profit!

COBBY: A lot of people are quite prepared go without it (their beer) for £10. A group of business-minded airmen formed a kind of ring to buy up any liquor they could get, and they finally started to get in chaps who normally would have drunk their beer. There were no worries; it was a case of 'pass your beer in this way and back comes your money that way'.

On the nights the beer was issued the Australian camps were invaded by hordes of thirsty Americans. To combat this, Cobby instituted spot checks on servicemen who were sending large amounts of money back to the Australian mainland. Hoarded money was brought back into circulation by an order substituting Dutch for Australian currency as the basis of exchange. Personnel found to have in their possession large amounts of money which they could not explain were removed from the area.

Mr Justice Barry was fair in his comments:

The conditions under which members of the forces serve in the Pacific area are harsh and monotonous. They do not resemble conditions obtaining in other theatres of war situated near cities and settled areas where in leave periods servicemen may have access in some degree to accustomed amenities.

My enquiries have shown that it has been an almost universal custom for officers of the RAAF, and doubtless other ranks, where opportunity presented to take liquor with them when leaving for operational areas in the Pacific outside the mainland. Technically, any member of the RAAF doing so is guilty of a breach of the order, but I am satisfied that the practice has no adverse effect upon discipline and no reasonable objection can be taken to it.

Barry was not so enthusiastic about exchanging liquor for equipment.

This might easily take on an aspect of commercialism and might encourage US servicemen to commit thefts—it cannot be approved.

Bruce, the commanding officer of 457 Squadron, was not much interested in alcohol and often other officers would drink his ration. If he had a visitor and found that his bottles had gone he would borrow another officer's bottle, but always replace it.

Clive always had a ready supply of liquor but Bruce confirmed that rather than sell it he used it to barter with the Americans to acquire better facilities for the Spitfire squadrons:

When we first arrived at Morotai, we had a campsite allocated to us that you wouldn't have put a dog kennel on.

It was rough ground that was uneven. There was scrub around it. It was anything but ideal for a good campsite and, within a matter of a day or so, three or four bulldozers arrived. And the bulldozers cleared that campsite and they pushed mounds up so that our tents were raised eighteen inches above the rest of the area. It became just an ideal campsite. And Clive did that, not only for 457 Squadron but for the other squadrons under his command.

We finished up with possibly one of the best campsites on that island. And it was all due to the work that the American bulldozers did. Now, how did he get the American bulldozers over there? He got them over there by giving them some grog.

He didn't sell it to them. He gave it to them. Whether he sold any grog or not, I don't know. I don't think he did. He wasn't interested in a few bob. He would rather have kept the bottle and drunk it than sell it. I can't imagine Clive ever selling a bottle.

According to Bruce, Clive spent his own money on providing a bar and recreational area where the squadron used to entertain nurses from the local hospital. Clive would often drop in for a drink and dinner at the mess. As Bruce recalled:

We had the best mess of any. We had a set of people that knew how to make a mess, and they'd have it decorated with a bit of palm trees, but our parties were always exceptional.

There were always girls from the hospital there, Teddy Sly made sure of that. He used to borrow the ambulance and he would tell me that my responsibility was to look after the Matron. If there were nurses in the mess he would be cordial to them but preferred to talk to the other pilots.

He'd stand over at the bar and fellows, of course, wanted to talk to Clive, wanted him to be there. I think they felt they could learn something. He'd talk about his flying but not stupidly. He would talk from the point of view of instructing and it was of help to them. He didn't shoot a line. He didn't pull any punches and he would talk about his deflection shooting and the importance of it.

Bruce was not much for long drinking sessions, and often preferred the company of his Alsatian dog, so he would slip away to his tent to have a quiet snooze.

But when Clive came down to our mess, usually by about 10.00, he would look around and he said, 'Where's that bloody CO? His dog's not here, he must be in his tent. Go and get him!'

Once, I knew all the boys were around him and I knew that he wouldn't miss me and I knew it was going to be a late night. Normally if there was flying the next day the take off time would be 7.30 am. As a punishment he ordered that we take off at six o'clock sharp. It was his way of showing us who was the boss.

Other officers, like Dick Cresswell, had heard of Caldwell's liquor trading and tried to warn him of the consequences.

I went across to Morotai to see Air Commodore Cobby.

Cobby said, 'We've got a problem. How well do you know Caldwell?'

'I know him quite well.'

'We know about Caldwell trading in liquor. The boys aren't very happy at all. Can you see him?'

I went and saw Caldwell. He took no notice of my
request to at least give some of the liquor to the squadrons.
He said he couldn't care less. He's selling this on the black
market to the Americans all the time. A bottle of Scotch
then 12 shillings.

Gin and Scotch mostly were the things the Yanks liked
to get hold of.

The most damaging evidence against Clive came from his
batman, Leading Aircraftsman Kenneth Parker. Parker had
first met Clive in Darwin.

He testified he was in Clive's tent when he had said:

There is money to be made in liquor at Morotai and if you
would like to sell some for me you can make some money.

The enquiry was told that on Christmas Day 1944 three
Americans came to the headquarters of 80 Wing, and asked
Leading Aircraftsman Kenneth Parker for liquor. He went to
Group Captain Caldwell's quarters, and Caldwell handed him
two or three bottles of whisky, which it was agreed between
them should be sold at 75 guilders a bottle. That night Parker
sold the whisky at the agreed price, and handed Group
Captain Caldwell the money.

Parker received a ten per cent commission. Parker
continued to make sales on Group Captain Caldwell's behalf
until 12 January 1945, obtaining liquor for sale about three
or four times a week. During the Christmas period these sales
amounted to over 1000 guilders (about £155).

'There was never any secret,' said Clive, 'about my having and trading liquor in Morotai. A supply was brought to me by Leigh Bressey of the 380th Bomb Wing in Darwin in appreciation of earlier service in defence of his aerodrome.'

Parker, it transpired was not very reliable. On 12 January Clive gave him six bottles of whisky for sale. Instead of selling them Parker went out and got drunk with the Americans.

The Americans asked me to have a few drinks here and there, which I did, and I finished up in an advanced state of intoxication. I woke up the following morning and I was minus my wallet and I owed Group Captain Caldwell approximately 450 guilders.

He reported this misadventure to Clive. 'I am quite willing to settle that business with you Sir.'

'All right, if you give me £25 everything will be all right,' Clive had stated.

Parker testified, 'I had £20 in my pay book, and I paid him approximately £18. I paid him everything except the 10 guilders which I still owe him.'

Parker and Leading Aircraftsmen George Charter and John Fitzroy told how they organised a home delivery service touring various American camps first on foot carrying the liquor in haversacks and later in a jeep. At one camp, Parker waited in the jeep, while Charter and Fitzroy went into a tent. At this point they were sprung by two Americans wearing military police armbands.

One of them said to Charter, 'Pick up your boxes and come along to the office.' The MPs then handed them over to the RAAF service police.

When they were caught, Charter and Fitzroy had with them five bottles of gin and two bottles of whisky. Charter also had a bottle of 'jungle juice', a home brew liquor made in illegal stills. It could be made almost drinkable if mixed with orange juice.

Parker drove back to 80 Wing Headquarters, and dumped the remaining liquor in Charter's tent. When Charter and Fitzroy didn't turn up the next day, Clive surmised that they had been picked up. Parker suggested to Clive that the remaining liquor in Charter's tent should be removed and hidden in the bushes. Later on another officer, Squadron Leader Dixon, told him to remove the cases and hide them in a slit trench behind his tent. Parker said, 'I carried out this instruction, and covered them with a raincoat, and that was the last time I handled them.'

Not long after, Clive had a visit from the appropriately named Pilot Officer Albert Schweppes, Deputy Assistant Provost Marshal of the Service Police Unit who told him that Fitzroy and Charter had both made statements implicating him in the sale of liquor.

Clive said, 'I cannot explain this except that the airmen may have thought that by mentioning their commanding officer's name they would get off more lightly.'

Schweppes made a search and the incriminating liquor—58 bottles of whisky, gin and sherry—was found in the slit trench.

The investigation was starting to look like a comic opera.

Schweppes warned Clive that he was not obliged to answer any more questions and that his answers might be used in evidence.

SCHWEPPES: Did you instruct Corporal Parker to remove the liquor from your quarters this morning?
CALDWELL: Is anything I say now in any way off the record?
SCHWEPPES said: Definitely not.
CALDWELL: Well I don't think anything I say would help me.

Leading Aircraftsman Charter told of his meeting with Clive:
CHARTER: What liquor have you available for sale?
CALDWELL: What do you want?
CHARTER: I have some gin ordered.
CALDWELL: I haven't any gin now but I can get some.

An hour later, Charter returned to Clive's quarters, and found four bottles of gin wrapped up in paper.

It was the evidence of Parker, Charter and Fitzroy that was particularly damning. Parker said that he had received about £375 selling liquor for Clive. Mr Justice Barry stated:

From the evidence of these witnesses which I accept as truthful and as accurate as the imperfections of memory permit, it appears that Group Captain Caldwell received in respect of the sale of liquor through Parker, Fitzroy and Charter a sum of about £470.

Barry also gave details of Clive's financial dealings. From the time of his arrival in Morotai in December 1944 to his departure, he paid £1153 18s 5d into his bank account at the Bank of New South Wales in Mildura. In a sworn statement, Clive maintained that the money came from the sale of liquor and winnings at various gambling activities. Justice Barry said:

> I have no doubt that he gambled frequently and successfully for high stakes, and I am unable to say what portion of the sum of £1153 18s 5d represented his takings from the sale of liquor. Taking into consideration the two sales made personally . . . I consider that his estimate of £300 is conservative and that £475 is nearer the true sum derived from his trading activities.

Clive was not the only officer who carried liquor in service aircraft. At least 30 other officers and other ranks admitted to having imported alcohol, including the Air Officer Commanding of the First Tactical Air Force, Air Commodore Arthur Cobby, and other fighter pilots like Dick Cresswell, Wilf Arthur and Les Jackson. Although this was strictly a breach of the new Air Board Orders the authorities were not unduly concerned so long as the liquor was for the consumption of officers and their friends.

Bobby Gibbes had also faced the lesser charge of 'attempting to sell liquor': one bottle of whisky, one bottle of wine and two bottles of gin. Gibbes decided to plead guilty as he wanted the charges dealt with in Morotai.

He said:

> I did not view my misdemeanour very seriously . . . thinking that this was all a trifling affair I pleaded guilty to the three charges and advised the court that I had in fact sold two or three bottles of alcohol.

Bobby Gibbes was reduced in rank from Wing Commander to Flight Lieutenant. Air Commodore Cobby intervened immediately afterwards and restored Gibbes to the rank of Squadron Leader.

Clive, however, had never been one to take the simple action and was always ready to fight tooth and nail when he believed he had a grievance. Before the day of the court martial Clive had written to Cobby, asking that his commission be terminated. He also claimed that to his certain knowledge, a number of senior RAAF officers, including *officers senior to him*, had sold and traded liquor.

> My offence therefore seems venial and, while I quite understand that it is the intention to take disciplinary action against me, I feel entitled to ask you to protect me against discriminating punishment.

Cobby ordered him to name the other officers. In reply, he named, among others, Cobby! Caldwell had implicated his boss!

Clive described how, earlier in the year, during the visit of Air Commodore Francis Bladin to Morotai, a group of senior officers including Clive was playing poker in Cobby's quarters. The others included Air Commodore Bladin, Group Captain Bill Gibson, Wing Commander Morris Meyer and Flight

Lieutenant Frank Quinn. Late in the evening the pilot of Bladin's aircraft, Squadron Leader Colin Lindeman, came into the room and said:

> I haven't been able to do too well on the cigarettes. There's a shortage on the island and they're not anxious to trade. I've got some for you but there are still a couple of bottles of whisky that I couldn't do any good with. Shall I leave them here?

He put the bottles on the floor.

Clive further claimed that Cobby's Lockheed Hudson had just flown up from Melbourne with a load of liquor; that he had seen a flight of Kittyhawks fly from Noemfoor to Darwin laden with liquor hidden in every available space, and that he had seen a cheque written by Cobby for the liquor!

Clive's allegations that Cobby and Bladin were involved in liquor trading were strenuously denied. There was, said Mr Justice Barry, not a scintilla of evidence that they had been. It was also not true that Cobby had written a cheque to pay for liquor bought in Australia.

Responding to Clive's allegations, Air Commodore Bladin did not deny taking liquor to Morotai, and specified four bottles of whisky and four bottles of gin, but said he was absent from Australia when Air Board Order 'N' was made and did not know it was contrary to air force law.

Someone, however, had been using Air Commodore Bladin's aircraft for smuggling cigarettes into Australia. On 23 January 1945, four customs officers were tipped off that

Bladin's Hudson bomber which had just arrived at Essendon airport in Melbourne, might be carrying contraband cigarettes which had been placed on the aircraft in Morotai.

After all personnel had disembarked, a search found nothing on the plane. They then approached a hut on the airfield, where they heard the sounds of objects being hastily thrown up into the roof. In the roof space they found boxes containing 40 000 American cigarettes, some of which had been stained with hydraulic oil. It appeared that a number of air force personnel had been trying to rapidly conceal the evidence.

The suggestion was that the cigarettes had been carried in the bomb bay of the aircraft which often leaked hydraulic oil. But there was no direct evidence of this, nor that either Bladin or Wing Commander Lindeman knew that the cigarettes in the hut had been carried on the aircraft.

The alcohol obtained by Bladin was in the nature of 'comforts' and was to be distributed by him at his discretion. Both Bladin and Lindeman denied having exchanged whisky for cigarettes.

The court martial proceedings against Group Captain Caldwell, said Barry, were properly and justifiably taken. The AOC Air Commodore Cobby would have been wanting in his duty had he not preferred charges in respect of the investigation made by Flying Officer Schweppes, and there was no ground for any suggestion that there was any discrimination against Group Captain Caldwell.

Curiously, despite the fact that Clive had indicted Cobby there were no hard feelings. Barry reported:

The personal relationship between Air Commodore Cobby AOC and Group Captain Caldwell was one of mutual regard and esteem and there is no ground for any suggestion that any of the matters which went to the inquiry resulted from any clash between them.

It must have been humiliating for an airman of Cobby's stature to face an interrogation by an officer several ranks his junior.

That officer was Flight Lieutenant R G Pluck, who cross-examined Cobby about Caldwell, and also about Cobby's ability to command the wing.

PLUCK: Did you have an opportunity of seeing him, and forming an estimate of his services during the period he was under you?
COBBY: Yes. His operational services were outstanding, although there was not a great deal of opportunity for his particular aircraft. His administrative ability was very high. His wing was well organised.

Flight Lieutenant Pluck, who appeared for the prosecution, suggested that RAAF aircraft were being sent on spurious missions against the Japanese which were actually liquor running flights.

An operation had been mounted using Kittyhawks against Tanimbar Island north of Darwin, where the Japanese were believed to be hiding out, and being resupplied at night by barges. Cobby was always a gentleman even under pressure.

PLUCK: Do you know about making a sweep on the Tanimbar island?

COBBY: Yes, that was a properly organised sweep.

PLUCK: Did you authorise that?

COBBY: In the initial discussion a week before it was pointed out that a lot of barge traffic was moving up at night in the area of Tanimbar island. There was a force of about 2500 (Japanese) in the area and we decided to strike. From memory, I think it was mostly ground installations and barges. The sweep was properly instituted and briefed after receiving intelligence reports.

PLUCK: Would it be correct to say that these sweeps had no operational value?

COBBY: No, that would be incorrect.

PLUCK: Would it be correct to say that they were primarily for the purpose of obtaining liquor in Darwin and bringing it back?

COBBY: Incorrect!

PLUCK: Would it be correct to say that the aircraft were stripped of armament in Darwin?

COBBY: No, incorrect. As a matter of fact on that sweep there was no need to use Kittyhawks to obtain liquor. They could use the Beauforts. We had three.

PLUCK: These aircraft after the sweep was concluded went off to Darwin?

COBBY: Yes, it is a geographical matter and the fact that petrol would be running low meant there was the danger of the aircraft going into the sea.

PLUCK: You know, of course, Air Commodore, that it has been suggested that the sweep was only an excuse for obtaining liquor?

COBBY: I read it in the press.

PLUCK: What would you say to that?

COBBY: It is impossible that anybody wanted an excuse to do that. There was no reason why we shouldn't get liquor from Darwin. We did not know that the famous or infamous 'N' order was in force and, as far as liquor requirements were concerned, we had no liquor from the canteen or anything else for six months, not even a piece of soap.

PLUCK: I suppose you will agree with me that the 'N' order 548 is very difficult to police?

COBBY: Not only difficult, but it was impossible to carry it out from the moment it was issued.

PLUCK: Impossible to carry out? In what way?

COBBY: Inasmuch as from a certain date the Air Force canteen was to supply liquor and therefore no more was to be taken into the country. It was directed against trading. However the canteen was not allowed to supply it and some of the canteen supplies did not get beyond Darwin.

In his report, Mr Justice Barry believed it important to quote Clive's statement, his own words, as to why he wanted to resign. Clive had said:

I am very anxious to return to civilian life, and continue as far as possible with the program of my life, and to achieve what my ambitions are. While we are at war, I am quite prepared to spend the whole of that time doing the best I can, providing there is a full field in which to do it but I do not want to spend another year away from my wife and my home—which has now started to add up to five years of almost constant absence, except for a few months, unless there is a justifiable purpose and a reason for my being away.

I just do not want to be a member of service wearing a uniform, sitting around and not doing anything to justify the continued absence. I wasted a year and I am not prepared to put in another year. That is the same style of thing and therefore as I feel that way it would be impossible for me to do a very good job at anything else in the Service. I stated that I believed there is no posting down here available to me in which I could really justify continuing in the service as a fairly senior officer.

Mr Justice Barry was also critical of Harry Cobby's two staff officers, Group Captains Gibson and Simms:

Group Captain Gibson is an officer who possesses great ability but, at times, through lack of application, falls down in his work. These lapses are not frequent but, unless he corrects this tendency, they may become part of his make up. He has a pleasant personality but at the same time is inclined to be somewhat arrogant and overbearing in dealing with juniors. This tends to cause friction which develops a lack of confidence by those officers in his ability.

On the celebrity circuit – Clive in Hollywood in 1943 at the house of the British actor Nigel Bruce. *Left to right*: Captain Cyril Wincott of the British Air Commission; Teddy Gwynn (a British character actor); Bunny Bruce (wife of Nigel Bruce). On the grass is the silent movie actor, Mary Pickford.

Squadron Leader R. S. McDonald (*left*) and Clive Caldwell in Darwin in 1943 – both men had just shot down a Japanese plane. (AWM NWA0403)

Spitfire pilots relaxing in Darwin, Clive Caldwell is standing at the rear.
(AWM NWA0404)

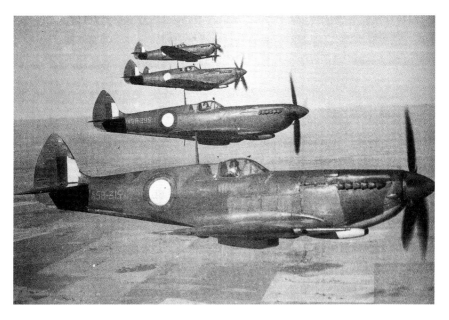

Spitfire Mark VIIIs flown by No 1 Fighter Wing in Darwin. They were a better
aircraft than the earlier MarkVs, but arrived too late to make any major impact.

Air Vice Marshal George Jones (*seated*), with senior RAAF officers in 1942. Chief of the Air Staff during World War II, he was regarded as an uninspiring leader but a capable administrator. Clive once said that if they were in the same room together he would have to be put into a cage! (AWM 128126)

Clive in his Spitfire, taking off from Livingstone in December 1944.

The face of the enemy: Captain Shunji Sasaki, the pilot of a Dinah operating from Timor. The plane was shot down by Squadron Leader Ken James.

Clive, his Spitfire and his score…
(AWM P02056.003)

A Mitsubishi Ki-46 Dinah. This fast reconnaissance aircraft flew many missions over the Northern Territory. Clive shot down a Dinah and counted three bodies in the water, even though the Dinah usually carried only two.

Clive and his personal Spitfire (Mark VIII), CR-C. He maintained two aircraft, in case one broke down. (AWM NWA0349)

At a makeshift bar in Morotai, 1944. Clive enjoyed a drink with his men and, according to Neville Duke, had a ferocious ability at the bar.

Clive dressed as a fairy for his role in the concert party, being helped to 'fly' by fellow officers. The picture was probably taken at Livingstone in 1943.

Clive in his seventies, with his full complement of medals.

Actual gun camera footage of a Mitsubishi Dinah being attacked by a Spitfire flown by Squadron Leader Ken James.

A rare picture of Japanese crew members farewelling the Dinahs as they took off from Lautem in Timor to fly on reconnaissance missions over the Northern Territory.

A captured Zero in American markings, Clark Field, Manila 1945.

ANZAC HOUSE APPEAL
PIN-UP MAN CONTEST
●
AN OUTSTANDING FIGURE

Wing-Commander C. ("Killer")
CALDWELL
(Combined Services Women's
Auxiliary).

Man of	**An**
Action	**Air Killer**
against the	**Of Enemy**
Japanese	**Fliers**

· · ·   · · ·

●

In real life, Wing Commander Clive Caldwell, popularly known an admiringly referred to as " Killer "Caldwell, D.S.O., D.F.C. and bar, Polish Cro of Valour-

NOMINATED BY THE WOMENS AUXILIARY COMBINED SERVICE SUB-BRANCH R S S A I L A

●

Vote for
1 Killer Caldwell
BUY AND WEAR A BUTTON FOR "KILLER"

Inquiries: 5 BARRACK STREET, SYDNEY.   Phone B 2909.

Crows Nest News Print. XB 4491.

Clive became a pin-up to the many back home – but publicity like this made him squirm.

Group Captain Gibson was over-confident, capricious, tended to rash decisions and was not cooperative.

Group Captain Simms is an extremely efficient officer who has the unfortunate habit of rubbing people the wrong way. In the assessment of his capabilities as an officer it appears that Group Captain Simms was not cooperative and was difficult.

At headquarters Simms allegedly had a sign on his door which read:

I'M BUSY TOO
Unless It's Damned Urgent
Go Away And Come Back Later.

Mr Justice Barry was in two minds about the sign:

There is a conflict of interest as to whether it was displayed, but it must have been prepared for some purpose, and few will dissent from Air Vice Marshal's Bostock's opinion that it was undignified and in bad taste.

Then there was the profit and loss account of Wilf Arthur. Barry wrote:

Expenditure in the operations which were described in evidence by Group Captains Arthur and Caldwell and Squadron Leaders Gibbes, Waddy and Grace far exceeded the material damage inflicted on the enemy and from that standpoint they were wasteful. Such wastefulness is inherent in the tactical employment of air forces against small pockets of the enemy in a theatre of war such as the South-West Pacific.

Barry was satisfied that the motives of Arthur, Gibbes, Waddy, Ranger, Grace, Vanderfield and Harpham in applying for permission to resign their commissions were sincere and honest.

When the findings of the Barry Commission were released in September 1945, it did not make the front pages of the newspapers. There were some bigger stories around.

The full implications of the raids on Hiroshima and Nagasaki were beginning to be realised—the world had suddenly entered the nuclear age, and 100 000 people could be killed with one bomb. In Europe, the vile practices of the Nazi Holocaust were exposed for all to see. In Australia, pitiful skeletons of men were returning from Japanese prison camps.

The war was over and most Australians had more important things on their minds. Did it really matter that a few air force officers had made a few bob out of selling grog to the Yanks?

The *Daily Telegraph* in Sydney said:

When all the enquiries and courts martial are finished, the RAAF should have a complete new deal. It is a badly run show and the fault is high up. The young men in the RAAF never had the chance which was given to the young RAF-ers in England. Our Air Force has been top heavy with mediocrities hanging on grimly to pension-less jobs, spending more time discouraging their juniors than inspiring efficiency.

Clive had the last word:

> . . . the dreamers of the RAAF headquarters and the incompetence of HQ TAF fed their ignorance and vanity by calling for these nonsensical operations for their own advancement and personal aggrandisement, which finally led to what was called the Mutiny of Morotai.

It has continued to be a widely held belief that members of the RAAF, during the years of the conflict in the South-West Pacific, were not well-served by the highest ranks. In 2001, John Coates wrote in an introduction to a brief account of the RAAF in action against Japan that:

> . . . it is impossible to separate the courage and excellence of its pilots and crew from the chronic derangement of its leadership. A melancholy series of command blunders put the service at the mercy of badly considered, bizarre decisions that stemmed from the top.

The heresy hunt

The enquiry over, it was four months before Clive finally faced his court martial which was reconvened at the RAAF No 2 Personnel Depot at Bradfield Park in Sydney.

Clive was not allowed to demobilise when the war ended; he had to remain in the air force until his court martial took place.

On 15 November 1945 the Department of Air issued a press release headed 'Caldwell Court Martial Soon'. It announced that Clive would be facing charges arising from alleged trading in liquor in operational areas, that the trial would be held in Sydney and that no date had yet been set. The press release explained that Clive was originally charged at Morotai in April:

> . . . but the trial was suspended because of operational commitments and the subsequent appointment . . . of Mr J

> V Barry . . . to . . . inquire into alleged liquor trading and
> dissatisfaction among senior RAAF officers of whom (Clive)
> was one.

Although this press release was written in November, and the
charge sheet had noted a trial date of 15 December, that sheet
was not signed until 24 December, nor the actual trial date
of 4 January 1946 set until 26 December.

The 'indecent haste' which Clive's counsel subsequently
deplored was the flurry of activity around Christmas 1945,
but charges had been pending since April that year. The
matter of Clive's court martial had been dragging on, both
sides determined to see it to a conclusion.

The court martial opened on 4 January 1946, but Clive's
defence counsel, Mr J E Cassidy KC, successfully applied for
an adjournment, arguing that there had been five different
charges sheets preferred against Clive since he had first been
arraigned, the latest as recently as 28 December.

There was, he claimed, an 'indecent haste on the part of
someone' to push this matter ahead. This did not given the
defence enough time to prepare its case.

Five charges had first been laid against Clive on 10 April
1945 and summary evidence had been taken on 11 April. On
16 April, five slightly different charges had been made, and a
subsequent field general court martial convened for 18 April.
Because the defending officer, Flight Lieutenant John
Davoren, was unable to attend on that date, it did not start
until 21 April. Operational requirements made it impossible
to for the court to sit and, on that date, Clive was released

from arrest 'without prejudice to re-arrest'. The matter was now dissolved.

Following Barry's report on the enquiry into all the matters surrounding Clive's case, a further five charges were laid on 16 October 1945, slightly different again. Cassidy was appalled that fifteen different charges had been made over eight months and that the four charges now being answered, again slightly changed from October's five, were signed as recently as 24 December.

Cassidy said that to ask a man, even if he were a humble airman, to defend himself on a new charge promulgated on 28 December and served upon him was extraordinary:

> . . . a convening order might easily have been made to have presented what is an indelicate and indecent haste without mentioning anything about the merits of a heresy hunt against Group Captain Caldwell.

There was also the problem of the availability of witnesses at such short notice.

Clive's case was adjourned until 16 January 1946.

Each charge was against Clive Robertson Caldwell's 'Conduct to the Prejudice of Good Order and Air Force Discipline'.

The specific incidents were:

1. At Morotai Island between 22 December 1944 and 15 February 1945 when officer commanding No 80 (Fighter) Wing headquarters improperly and contrary to his duty

engaged in the selling of alcoholic liquor namely whisky and gin through the agency of No 5139 Corporal Parker K. an airman member of No 110 Fighter Control Unit, a unit under the command of No 80 (Fighter Wing) headquarters contrary to paragraph 7 of Air Board Orders 'N' 548 of 1944.

2. At Morotai Island about the end of February 1945, when officer commanding No 80 (Fighter) Wing headquarters improperly and contrary to his duty sold alcoholic liquor namely four bottles of gin to No 146207 LAC Charter GC an airman member of No 110 Mobile Fighter Control unit, a unit under the command of No 80 (Fighter Wing) Headquarters contrary to paragraph 7 of ABO 'N' 548 of 1944.

3. At Morotai Island about the end of February 1945 when officer commanding No 80 (Fighter Wing) Headquarters improperly and contrary to his duty sold alcoholic liquor namely two bottles of whisky to No 146207 LAC Charter GC an airman member of No 110 Mobile Fighter Control Unit under the control of No 80 (Fighter Wing) Headquarters contrary to paragraph 7 of ABO 'N' 548 of 1944.

4. At Morotai Island on or about 31 March 1945 and 1 April 1945 when commanding officer No 80 (Fighter Wing) Headquarters, improperly and contrary to his duty engaged in the selling of alcoholic liquor, namely whisky and gin through the agency of No 146207 LAC Charter GC an airman member of No 110 Mobile Fighter Control Unit, a unit under the command of No 80 (Fighter Wing)

Headquarters contrary to paragraph 7 of ABO 'N' 548 of
1944.

Clive's counsel gained permission for the first charge to be
heard before a full plea be entered.

Clive pleaded not guilty.

In Clive's statement, which was read to the court, he did not
deny importing liquor to Morotai, but said he had used it to
barter with the Americans for equipment so that he could set
up a proper camp. Among other things, he said, they had
acquired seven large tanks, two water pumps, timber, water
piping joints and tentage. He had also the use for long periods
of drilling machines, boring plants, bulldozers, automated
compressed-air hammers and heavy motor transport for haulage
of water and carriage of personnel. The value ran into thousands
of pounds; he had acquired it for a few bottles of liquor.

The prosecution's case still hinged on the damning
evidence given by Kenneth Parker, Clive's batman and George
Charter. Cassidy conducted a searching cross examination of
Parker who had admitted that he was so drunk he could not
remember what happened.

> CASSIDY: It didn't take you long to find out that trading
> in liquor (in Morotai) was prevalent?
> PARKER: No, it didn't take me long.
> CASSIDY: In fact it was hitting you in the eye?
> PARKER: Yes.
> CASSIDY: I think that there was a fair market price fixed
> at about 75 guilders for whisky and 60 for gin?

PARKER: That was the usual price.

CASSIDY: You couldn't blame anyone for wanting beer up there?

PARKER: No.

CASSIDY: You will remember that around about 12 January that there were six bottles of Scotch which disappeared?

PARKER: I don't know the amount but some disappeared.

CASSIDY: And Group Captain Caldwell was pretty angry about that?

PARKER: Yes, he was annoyed.

CASSIDY: I think you said that you were a steward—a ship's steward—before you joined the Air Force?

PARKER: Yes.

CASSIDY: And I suppose that is a job where you learn to be very confidential about other people's business, is it not?

PARKER: That's right.

CASSIDY: And you have always endeavoured to be extremely confidential about your master's business?

PARKER: That is right.

CASSIDY:And you applied that same outlook to your service in the Air Force did you not?

PARKER: Yes.

CASSIDY: You told the court this morning that you got into an advanced state of intoxication and woke up the following morning?

PARKER: That is right.

CASSIDY: You didn't mention this morning that you had been in a brawl?

PARKER: No, I never thought anything about that.

CASSIDY: Why?

PARKER: It never occurred to me.

CASSIDY: It never occurred to you (dramatic pause) I see. Doesn't it seem strange to you that you should forget being knocked about—it's not the kind of thing you forget?

PARKER: No it's not.

CASSIDY: Although you described getting drunk you don't remember the brawl?

PARKER: I never gave it a thought.

CASSIDY: I suppose you have been drunk before?

PARKER: On occasions.

Clive's version of the events were quite different. He said that it had been Parker who had first approached *him* with the suggestion that he could sell some liquor for cash.

A small quantity of liquor was sold through LAC Parker. Such sales ceased when this airman was found very drunk in the company of two American soldiers one morning, they and others having used liquor taken from my store. I am informed that LAC Parker told the service police he was beaten up and robbed on that occasion. This is in direct contradiction to his statement at the time and the circumstances. Several witnesses were present and LAC Parker scouted (rejected) any suggestion that he had been subjected to ill treatment. He bore no marks on his face or above the waist and was most anxious to spend the rest of the day with his American friends, who were seen to be waiting for him just outside the camp.

If Air Vice Marshal Jones was keen to the make the charges stick, Clive was not going to go down without a fight. He said he had heard Jones say himself that his own pilot, Squadron Leader Upjohn, had carried liquor on his personal aircraft on occasions between August 1944 and May 1945 when he had been making duty flights to areas outside Australia.

However, the Chief of the Air Staff made no enquiries of Squadron Leader Upjohn, nor did he have any communication with Squadron Leader Upjohn's commanding officer.

Clive said:

> To my mind that indicates pretty clearly the real importance attached by the highest ranking Air Force authority of importing liquor to the islands and having sold it.

Clive was found guilty of the first charge. After consulting with his counsel he changed his plea to guilty to the fourth charge. As proposed earlier in the hearing, the second and third charges were not proceeded with. There was no point in prolonging the agony and Clive was anxious to get it over with.

Mr Cassidy, in his summing up, said that in deciding its sentence the tribunal was now charged with the very grave responsibility when prejudicing the career of a man who for over six years had been so good in character and achievement: 'I do ask the court to put out of its mind any savage approach to the question.'

Clive would probably have been promoted to the rank of air commodore in February, which meant that from February

1941 to February 1945 he would have progressed from the rank of flight lieutenant to air commodore. Cassidy said:

> Just let us look at the consequences which would follow reduction in rank to flight lieutenant. Punishments must always be directed to the offence which the individual has committed. In this air force, which is still young, who has added more to its permanent distinction than him? What names are there in our minds that are reigning greater tradition for the Air Force and greater things for the Australian Air Force throughout the world than what he did?
>
> In some Australians that see men rise there is a meanness of outlook that loves to find a chink in the armour of a great man. We have seen it with heroes of the past.
>
> Take Sir Charles Kingsford Smith who was attacked by some newspaper when in some bad weather he brought that plane that he loved, the *Southern Cross*, and deliberately landed it for stunt at a place called Coffee Royal. So that you get people who are ready, if a man makes a slip, to penalise him and advertise the chink in his armour. Let us approach the matter of punishment with a broader and more generous outlook.
>
> As I say, punishment varies with the individual. Reduction in rank to this man means he leaves the service where he has had such rapid promotion, leaves it as a flight lieutenant losing the rank that was given to him. In conclusion I say to the court this one point only— punishment is something that must be considered with regard to a particular case. It is an unusual case. It is one

of two cases only in regard to all the trading that took place there. Let us not kill our heroes. Let his reputation remain, I think, with what to him is unfortunate, a reprimand.

Mr Cassidy's eloquent summing up was to no avail. On 18 January 1946 the president of the court martial, Air Vice Marshal S J Goble, asked Clive to stand to attention as he read out the sentence, that: 'Squadron Leader Acting Group Captain Clive Robertson Caldwell be reduced to the rank of Flight Lieutenant'.

Clive later quietly left the service, bitter and humiliated. After the war he was to write:

There was never any secret about my having and trading liquor in Morotai. By reason of my liquor supplies, some 3000 personnel lived in healthier circumstances, sanity and comfort than would otherwise have been the case.

Back to business

Clive's war ended quietly. The last time he sat at the controls of a service aircraft was a routine flight in a Wirraway trainer from Parkes in New South Wales on 26 October 1945. It was an ignominious end to a distinguished flying career. The Wirraway was a sturdy, unglamorous machine, which did not quite have the allure of the Spitfire.

Not that anyone could ever see Clive remaining in the air force in peacetime. He would never have been satisfied joining the shiny bum brigade. The best times had been in the Middle East. His time in Darwin had been tedious and frustrating, and when the Japanese raids petered out, there was not a lot to do.

Bruce Watson recalled:

He'd had that exciting experience of the Middle East where he had a tremendous number of victories. If he'd been given the opportunity he could have been equal to any fighter ace. But he found the operations back here very unsatisfactory.

He was only happy really when he was stepping out of a Spitfire and when he'd achieved something for the war effort.

Even before the war in the Pacific was over, Clive had been approached to see if he would consider running for the New South Wales State Parliament. On 20 April 1944, the President of the Liberal Democratic Party of Australia, Mr E K White, had written to Clive asking him to consider going into politics.

> I would be glad if you could see your way clear to accept the candidature for one of the electorates. The Illawarra area has been suggested as one in which you would have every chance of success.

Clive's comment was, 'Cannot accept in view of absence on operations'. After the war he was approached by Prime Minister Robert Menzies to stand for the Liberal Party. Certainly, if these idle jottings from the 1980s are considered, it is not difficult to see where Clive stood on the political spectrum:

> As we know idleness and despair are the twin curses of the unemployed. This breeds crime. If there is a hope it is the principle of self-help. Therefore the government should do more to help such people start helping themselves.
>
> Certainly not discourage employment by penalising the employed with a special tax for doing so. Here in Australia we must take special care, because life here at the bottom

of the world is different to that outside, and will need to change if we are to maintain a semblance of what we should have as a way of life.

Too many people have been encouraged to go far too long without work and more leave school and are likewise encouraged never to work but to be content to continue on as the country's charity ward. We could afford three years national service better than we can afford a flock of F/A 18s some of which are flown by clowns at the orders of fools. The Aussie principal by the unions is that a one-man job is better handled by five members of the same union.

Although he had distanced himself from the RAAF, Clive maintained a passing interest in aviation. In 1946 he had returned to the Philippines and bought five war surplus Stinson L 5 aircraft which had been left behind by the departing Americans. He sold all but one, which he kept at Mascot aerodrome in Sydney for own personal use.

The little Stinson was the equivalent of a flying jeep, and had been used for aerial spotting and forward air control. It was only a two-seater, with the passenger seated behind the pilot. He and Jean used to fly down to the Illabo property and land on the grass strip. After years of separation, at last she could be alone with her man. She loved sitting behind Clive in the noisy little Stinson gazing down on the dry bush.

In 1946 pilots were ten a penny and jobs in aviation scarce. Clive decided to go into business and started looking around for partners.

Before the war, Clive had befriended the pastoralist George

Falkiner who ran a big merino and cotton property at Haddon Rig near Warren in New South Wales. They went into business together as Falkiner-Caldwell, importing fabrics from overseas. Initially the company supplied wool to the English mills then re-imported the woven cloth which they sold to department stores. Later the company began importing lining fabrics for men's suits.

Although the company was later to provide Clive with a comfortable living, the early days were not all plain sailing. In 1952 the company was importing a non-woven interlining from Germany which they supplied to Myers. The contract fell through and the company nearly went broke.

George Falkiner had also bought one of the surplus Stinsons. On one occasion he was entertaining a visitor from America and asked Clive to take him for a flight in his aeroplane.

Clive, what are you doing this afternoon?

Well, I don't know. Why?

I've got this friend out from the States. Would you take him and give him a buzz around Sydney in my plane? He does fly, so you should let him have a go if he wants.

The American, however, was not quite as proficient a pilot as Falkiner had been led to believe. On approach to the runway he clipped some pine trees and ripped off the undercarriage. The Stinson ended up on its belly in the middle of the runway and was extensively damaged, although neither Clive nor his passenger was hurt.

Clive rang Falkiner and reported: 'Your bloody mate can't fly and your aircraft's all over Mascot aerodrome.'

Clive's company established its headquarters at 50 York Street in Sydney in the heart of Sydney's garment industry. Graham Masters was 23 when he joined the company in 1969. The job interview took the form of informal drinks at the nearby Occidental Hotel, one of Clive's favourite watering holes:

> He was certainly a man's man. He he was a very tough boss, but extremely fair. The sort of guy that if you made a mistake, you'd be invited in for the cup of tea and shut the door, and he'd tear bloody strips off you and that's where it would finish.
>
> He was a good businessman. He certainly kept his eye on the ball. He had his policies that had to be adhered to. He was very, very tight on making people pay for things that they bought. He had no hesitation at all of lining somebody up if they tried to jink him or something like that, but he'd be the very first person, if somebody came in and said, 'Look, I'm in a bit of strife and this is how I'm going to get out of it,' he'd support him to the hilt. But the people who tried to duck and weave and hide and that sort of thing, he crashed down on them with all guns blazing.

Graham was vaguely aware of what he had done in the war, but Clive was reluctant to talk about the past: 'He would say that it was a great waste of time and human life, and that he was not really interested.'

Like many who met Clive for the first time, Graham got the impression that Clive put people on trial before he trusted them: 'He was suspicious of people I think. In actual fact, he was probably a little bit shy.'

Like many companies in the rag trade, the firm moved its headquarters south to Surry Hills, the new hub of the garment industry. The business was humming along. It employed sixteen people including shipping clerks, invoice typists and storemen. Clive ran the firm with military precision. He insisted that the office staff wore jackets and ties and that the female employees came to work neatly dressed. He frowned at mini-skirts. From his office window, Clive could see men running across the street carrying rolls of fabric on their shoulders. It was a close-knit working community of machinists, cutters and cloth buyers.

He was a bit old school, a bit Victorian, but he had pride in the business and enjoyed watching it run properly. He was known to be a fair employer who didn't try to squeeze every ounce out for himself. The staff received a bonus if times were good; if they were bad they did not get one. It was a bit like his days in the desert when he had handed out medals. Some of the staff occasionally felt they were on parade and should be standing to attention.

When well beyond the normal age for retirement, Clive was to hand over control of the company to Graham:

He gave me the baton to run the place and was coming in two days a week and something would go wrong and, well,

I'd have to stand up to him, which was quite difficult to do, actually.

'Fair enough,' he'd say, 'fair enough, righto.'

Drawing the blinds

After the war Clive was keen to draw down the blinds on his war career and refused many would-be biographers.

When journalists persuaded him to talk the conversation quickly came round to the Morotai Mutiny, his court martial, the Barry enquiry and his bitterness towards George Jones.

In 1989 the whole thing blew up again when George Jones made public his version of the story. Clive wrote to his solicitor:

> Here are some quick rough notes which may help you to understand George Jones's views on me. To him I was always at fault it seems. In 1945/46 I cared little about his views or sayings having better things to do. But now this meagre little type pursues me across the generation gaps with his petty inaccuracies and nonsense which I find damaging at this stage of life and feel that he should be tested to prove what the article says.
>
> It always seemed to me during the various courts martial

on which I served (either as president or accused) that there were two conditions. Legal guilt and moral culpability. They're not always the same. I'm not trying to instruct you in the legal niceties as attending to them is part of your job. However I want this officially rescinded and my good name cleared of this impropriety Jones raked up and falsely laid on me.

In 1988, the distinguished military historian, George Odgers, produced a novel, *Aces Wild*, basing it on the true events of the Morotai Mutiny. In the book Harry Cobby becomes Air Commodore Arnold Tremayne Blandy and Caldwell is Group Captain David Miller.

Clive went into the attack with all guns blazing:

This imaginative tale is incorporated in many pages of confusion and complexity; the definitions and convoluted deeming situations are difficult to follow and in many respects are very close to being incomprehensible—even to an actual player in the events which albeit were however small a bubble nevertheless a part of the greatest military adventure in history. Why is it that those who have no knowledge of events insist on writing what purports to be a reasonable presentation of them?

For the last ten years of his life, with time on his hands, Clive was drinking heavily and this was occasionally to bring him into conflict with the authorities.

He would put in a couple of hours at the office then

adjourn for lunch to the Sydney Golf Club or the Royal Automobile Club in Macquarie Street.

Returning from a long lunch at the golf club one day, Clive was driving his Mercedes when it ran off the road, mounted the footpath and hit a tree in New South Head Road. Bruce Watson says the mark on the tree is still visible.

> The lights changed on him and he got caught and he was going so quickly that he swung across, mounted the footpath and the Mercedes was impaled on the tree.

Clive got out of the car, locked it up, and caught a taxi home. A half an hour later, the police arrived, and asked him if he had been drinking. He told them that to steady his nerves he had drunk a couple of stiff Scotches when he first got home.

> He said, 'Well, what the hell would you do if you had an accident like that? Wouldn't you have a drink?'

The police had to accept that Clive wasn't driving under the influence:

> He got away with it. No one else was involved, but someone reported it and, of course, there was the Mercedes on the footpath with its bonnet embedded in the tree and hundreds of dollars worth of damage, and Clive was sitting at home having a Scotch.

On another occasion Clive failed to stop at the junction of

Riley Street and Foveaux Street and hit a taxi. The taxi careered across the road, and came to rest against a building on the other side of the road. Clive walked into the corner pub and drank four straight double whiskies.

The police arrived and found Clive at the bar doing a plausible imitation of a man in shock.

'Have you been drinking Mr Caldwell?' enquired one of the policemen.

'Bloody oath I've been drinking', said Clive. 'Just scared the shit out of myself.'

Once again Clive got away with it. Fortunately for him the introduction of the breathalyser was some years away. Bruce Watson was often invited to lunch but as in his wartime days had never been a drinking man.

When I first knew Clive, he was always in the Automobile Club. And he was always there every lunch. And lunch, of course, was always a liquid lunch.

After the war when I was working in the city, Clive invited me down a couple of times to lunch at the Automobile Club. And I met George Falkiner; he was very, very pleasant, but it was never lunch.

We never left the top bar.

So I just said to Clive one day, 'Clive, thank you. I do appreciate your invitations, but I can't drink like that. I'm a very poor drinker. I'm of no value up there whatsoever.'

If Clive played golf it was rarely more than nine holes. Bruce Watson said:

He would go down to the first tee and he would play a shot off the first tee with an iron and usually, the ball would finish up somewhere in the rough.

He'd say, 'That's enough for today.' And he'd walk back to the bar.

There were other incidents which today would be tantamount to road rage. One day in Double Bay, Clive had angry words with another driver who tried to throw a punch at him through the open window of Clive's Jaguar.

Clive ducked and grabbed the man's arm pulling him into the car, then wound up the electric windows trapping his head which he then proceeded to pummel. It was not in any sense behaviour befitting a Group Captain in the RAAF or a city businessman; but then, Clive had always been a fighter; no quarter was asked for and none given.

Even late in life Clive maintained his passion for firearms and rarely went anywhere without a pistol, even if he was going out to dinner. His favourite gun was a 9 mm Biretta automatic, the type favoured by James Bond.

Graham Masters didn't like it:

There was a hair trigger on the bloody thing and it used to scare the hell out of me because I thought, 'Oh, God! Somebody's going to upset him one night and he's going to shoot somebody.'

One night at a dinner party at a friend's house, the Biretta slipped out of Clive's pocket and onto the floor. The hostess tactfully picked it up and handed it back to him. Why Clive needed to carry his 'equaliser' as he called it, is anyone's guess, but there is no record of him ever using it.

The Biretta was the only gun for which he owned a licence but hidden about the house, in the safe at his office, and in his locker at the golf club there was a veritable arsenal of weapons. Clive owned 20 guns including a German machine pistol in a wooden holster, a .44 Smith and Wesson, two army issue .45s and a classic Colt .45 that had been made in 1896. There were M 16 automatics, Lee Enfield .303s, a double barrelled shotgun and a Winchester rifle. There was also a considerable amount of ammunition, some of it World War II vintage.

When the couple visited the property at Illabo Clive would take his weapons out to the dam and set up some old cans for shooting practice. Jean would accompany him but she was not enthusiastic about firearms.

Bruce Watson paid a visit to the property and went for a stroll with Clive, who was carrying his Colt .45 with him.

A crow was flying slowly across the sky.

Clive said, 'Jeez, I'll get that bloody crow,' and yanked the revolver out of its holster like Billy the Kid.

. . . and he just followed it for a few seconds and put the deflection on it and fired. And he didn't knock it down, but he knocked a lot of feathers off it.

Most shooters would not have been able to hit the bird with a shotgun let alone a single bullet, but Clive was quite annoyed that he had only winged it:

He came in and said to Jean, 'I just missed a damn crow today. I should have knocked him down, but I only knocked the feathers off it.' He was a remarkable shot.

After Clive died, Jean Caldwell rang Graham Masters and asked him to dispose of the guns. There had been a number of amnesties where guns could be handed in at the police station with no questions asked, but this time had now passed.

By now the authorities would have taken a dim view of a private armoury as big as Clive's.

Mrs Caldwell called me up to the den, and she said, 'Graham, these guns, I don't want them in the house. I've always detested them. Clive always wanted me to shoot.' And he'd taught her how to shoot with the Biretta, which was the only licensed gun he had.

And I said, 'Well, um, what are we going to do with them? Will we hand them over to the police?'

She said, 'I don't care. I just want to get rid of them.'

Masters rang a police ballistics expert who said he would drop round to the office to inspect the guns. Even he was not quite prepared for such an extensive collection. 'The policeman walked into the office, took one look and said, "Holy Jesus!"'

Clive's personal armoury was quietly handed over to the New South Wales police and nothing more was heard about it.

Like many pilots, Clive was a nervous passenger. Once he and Graham Masters flew to Melbourne on a regular commercial flight.

Sitting next to him in the plane Graham noticed that Clive was looking uncomfortable and fidgeting.

And I said, 'You all right?'
Clive said, 'I will be, once he gets this bloody thing up in the air. Anything I can't keep my own hands on, I'm nervous all right, particularly aeroplanes.'

As the plane started accelerating down the runway, Graham, noticed that Clive was counting.

Clive said, 'Yep. If it goes past another three seconds, and we're still on the ground we're in trouble.'
He was a nervous flyer when he wasn't at the controls.

For the last fifteen years of his life Clive was reluctant to travel overseas. In the late 1980s he reluctantly agreed to go to America to the 'Gathering of Eagles', a reunion of famous fighter pilots, but only if he travelled first class and stayed at a good hotel. He enjoyed it while he was there but came back exhausted. It was his last big trip.

For the last 40 years of their life together, the Caldwells settled in Bellevue Hill in a graceful white house with views of Sydney Harbour.
Clive was often invited to Air Force functions, but usually avoided them. When it was suggested that an organisation was formed to honour those who had flown the Spitfire he

was characteristically difficult about it and suggested that rather than being called the Spitfire Association it should be called the Number One Fighter Wing Association.

Clive disassociated himself from flying and preferred to maintain a low profile but, in 1961, he gave a rare television interview to the ABC's 'Four Corners' which showed what a shy man he was. The interviewer, Michael Charlton, had a difficult time prizing anything out of him.

By the 1960s the jet age had arrived and most Spitfires had been scrapped. But two of the Darwin Spitfire Mark VIIIs had survived and had been dumped on the edge of Bankstown aerodrome minus their wings and propellers. This was used as backdrop to the interview.

Clive, looking immaculate in a well-cut suit, walked self-consciously around the derelict fuselages with a cigarette in his hand, Charlton holding a microphone.

CHARLTON: Makes you sad to see these aircraft lying on the ground in someone's backyard?
CLIVE: Well, it is a bit sad. I think they deserve better than this.
CHARLTON: It must bring back a few memories for you when you see them?
CLIVE: They'd probably have been with No 80 Fighter Wing at Darwin.

Clive pulled back the sliding canopy and Charlton persuaded him to climb into the cockpit:

CHARLTON: How does a big tall fellow like you get into one of these things? How does it feel after all this time?
CLIVE: A little strange
CHARLTON: What were you thinking when you pushed back that hood just now?

Clive looked around him in the cockpit and placed his hand on the control column.

CLIVE: Well gun button, guns on, all guns, no noise.

Walking away from the Spitfire, he slapped the side of the engine and ran his hands along it. 'I had my own plane but I don't fly any more. There's no thrill in it for me these days.' Looking over his shoulder at the aircraft, he said: 'But they're a beautiful thing in the air, and they still look the part.'

In March 1993, Clive called Graham Masters to tell him that he had been diagnosed with prostate cancer.

Clive said, 'Jean and I have been talking and we've had to make some big decisions. Jean and I want to bail out of the business and we'd like you to take it over.'

Graham was enthusiastic about the prospect of taking over. Clive said:

'Well, all right, we'll start. We'll put the ball in play and start sort of seeing how we're going to do it.'

Clive made arrangements for Graham to take over the company at the beginning of the next financial year. But for the next twelve months Clive was continually in and out of hospital and it was obvious he was going downhill. The operation for prostate cancer was unsuccessful and the cancer had spread throughout his body. The chemotherapy treatment left him weak and miserable. Friends who came to visit him at St Vincents Hospital were shocked at how frail he looked, although he could still make jokes about his predicament.

Graham found it deeply disturbing to see Clive deteriorating. By now he would rarely come to the office so Graham used to visit him at his home in Bellevue Hill and have a whisky with him in his den.

> It was very, very sad to see a guy going like that. I can only say, thank God he didn't last all that long.
>
> I learned a lot from the man and totally respected him. He was good to me, as was Mrs Caldwell, certainly. When he was passing away, he left a lot for me to do, looking after Mrs Caldwell.

Drifting in and out of consciousness Clive looked back on his life:

> Memories flowed by like a long chain of bubbles on the surface of a stream steering their own way down the years sometimes breaking almost as I caught sight of them sometimes sailing; stones and sticks of fixed events in my life and riding on out of sight AS I MUST DO TOO. Tiny

unimportant details stood out with clarity—the shadow of my aircraft as I land on the desert landing ground, the smell of roast pork when they dragged old T from the flames of his burning aircraft at Hanish; the flotilla of small boats following our own ships down Sydney Harbour as a farewell.

For Jean it was a wretched time and she hated seeing the old warrior brought so low. On one of her last visits Clive made a wan attempt at humour. 'Put me into an old truck and send me off', he said.

Graham Masters last saw Clive the day before he died.

I didn't think he was going to pass away at that particular time, but when I arrived at the hospital that afternoon, Mrs Caldwell was there and she came out to me and she burst into tears and she said, 'They told me Clive doesn't have a lot of time left.' She said, 'I can't go back in the room now, Graham. I want to go for a walk, if you don't mind. I don't want him to see me upset.'

Clive Caldwell died on 5 August 1994. At his request the funeral was a quiet affair. Months later, Jean spoke to one of the stewards at the Royal Sydney Golf Club where Clive had spent so many happy hours. 'I miss him so much,' he said 'He was a very strong man and he used to keep us all in order. And that's what we need now.'

Clive did not get a state funeral; that honour was reserved for cricket players and politicians. Only the Northern Territory government held an adjournment to record his passing.

In a speech to the house, Shane Stone, the chief minister, said, 'He was the most successful fighter pilot in World War II and possibly the most successful combatant to serve in this area.'

The newspaper obituaries celebrated Clive's fine record as a fighter pilot and there was hardly a mention of his battles with the higher echelon of the RAAF not to mention the liquor trading and the court martial—if that even mattered any more.

There had been two generations of fighter pilots since Clive had flown Spitfires. The first Gulf War had just finished and, as Clive had predicted in 1941, Islamic militants were to bring a new form of terror to the world.

At the time Clive died, only one airworthy Spitfire survived in Australia of the 656 which had been supplied from Britain, lovingly maintained like a vintage car by sentimental enthusiasts. Fighter aircraft were now spiky and ugly.

The fighter pilots of the 1990s flew their planes with the help of computers and played loud rock music in their headphones. A robot voice told them when to fire their missiles, then they went out with their girlfriends to drink martinis in air-conditioned bars. War had become impersonal; you never saw the enemy and pilots didn't dog-fight any more. Fighter pilots were now cool and sophisticated and although the computers helped them to hit their targets they still missed occasionally. It was only a matter of time before unmanned aircraft took over the job completely.

By the early years of the 21st century, most of Caldwell's contemporaries were dead. Three of his fellow officers have the last word.

Dick Cresswell:

Caldwell loved the publicity. He wanted to be in the forefront the whole time. Once he became the top ace in Australia, he became the media's leading light. He loved the press and the press loved him. All these victories . . . an extraordinary man. Basically a nice bloke but towards the end he drank too much.

Bobby Gibbes:

I knew him quite well. Not on a friendship deal. He was very sure of himself all the time.

What do you think he was cranky later in life?

He was cranky about being court martialled. I was court martialled at the same time. I deserved to be.

What did you mean by that? A few bottles of gin?

Yes. It seemed a bit trivial after what we'd both been through.

Bruce Watson:

He was a fine leader, a remarkable shot, and a good friend.

Appendix

RECORD OF SERVICE OF ACTING GROUP CAPTAIN
CLIVE ROBERTSON CALDWELL (402107)

Date of birth: 28.7.1910

Date of enlistment: 25.5.1940

Promotions:

    Leading Aircraftsman 22.7.40

    Pilot Officer 12.1.41

    Flying Officer 12.7.41

    Acting Flight Lieutenant 25.9.41

    Acting Squadron Leader 6.1.42

    Temporary Flight Lieutenant 1.10.42

    Acting Wing Commander 1.1.43

    Temporary Squadron Leader 1.7.44

    Acting Group Captain 1.8.44

Appointments:

    Commanding Officer No. 112 Sqdn. RAF
    21.12.41–6.5.42

Wing Leader No 1 Fighter Wing 23.11.42–26.9.43
T/C.O. No 1 Fighter Wing 26.6.43–26.9.43
Chief Instructor No 2 OTU 27.9.43–26.9.43
C.O. No 80 Fighter Wing HQ 25.10.44–2.5.45

Postings

No 2 RD	27.5.40 No 1 (P) Course
No 1 ITS	10.6.40 No 1 (P) Course
No 4 EFTS	25.7.40 No 1 (P) Course
No 2 SFTS	23.9.40 No 1 (P) Course
No 2 ED	31.1.41 On Draft No 1 for M.E.
Att. RAF Middle East	3.2.41 Flying
No 1 ED	17.9.42 On return from overseas
No 2 OTU	5.10.42 Flying Instructor
No 1 Fighter W HQ	23.11.42 Wing Leader
No 2 OTU	27.9.43 Chief Instructor
No 80 Wing HQ	7.5.44 Command
No 2 PD	3.5.45 Disposal

Honours and Awards:

Dinstinguished Service Order DFC and Bar, Polish Croix des Vaillants 1939–45 Star and rosette. Embarked for Middle East 3.2.41 Deplaned at Amberley Queensland ex U.K. and Canada on 14.9.42.

Total flying hours as at 31.12.44—1224

Extracts from citations

Flight Lieutenant CR Caldwell
—Distinguished Flying Cross

CITATION:

For courage, determination and devotion to duty. This officer has performed consistent and brilliant work in operations in various theatres of war in the Middle East. He has at all times shown dogged determination, great courage and a high devotion to duty which has proved an inspiration to his fellow pilots.

On one occasion in particular during a patrol over units of the Royal Navy, he was attacked by several Messerschmitt 109s. His aircraft was badly damaged while he himself received bullet wounds in the chest, shoulder and leg and shrapnel wounds in the face and side. Nevertheless he courageously returned to the attack and shot down one of the hostile aircraft, driving off another. It was felt that had his aircraft not been so extensively damaged and shot up, that the other Messerschmitt would probably not have escaped.

Bar to DFC

CITATION:

F/Lt Caldwell continues to take his toll of enemy aircraft. This officer has consistently participated in attacks on enemy ground forces and in many battles over the Libyan desert in the course of the present offensive personally accounting for seven more enemy aircraft.

He flies on every possible sortie against the enemy often leading our formations and displays at all times an aggressiveness of spirit and a determination and devotion to duty of the highest order.

On one occasion in particular, the flight of aircraft F/Lt Caldwell was leading engaged a greatly superior number of Junkers 87s and Me-109s over the battle area. In the fight which followed more than 20 of the enemy were destroyed.

In all F/Lt Caldwell has destroyed twelve enemy aircraft and shares in another, while he has probably destroyed and damaged almost as many more.

Polish Cross of Valour (Krzyz Walecznych)

CITATION:

In recognition of gallantry and courage displayed during air combats in the Middle East in 1941 and in 1942 when as commanding officer of 112 Squadron RAF to which Polish fighter pilots are attached, and in accordance with with Article 5 of the Order issued by the Polish Defence Council, on the 11th of August 1920 concerning the award of the Krzyz Walecznych and with article 2a of the Decree of the President of the Polish Republic,

I award the Krzyz Walecznych
To Clive Robertson Caldwell
Squadron Leader
Commander in Chief
General Sikorski

Distinguished Service Cross
Wing Commander Caldwell   22.6.43

CITATION:

Wing Commander Caldwell on completion of his flying training was posted overseas in January 1941, served with much distinction and was officially credited with the destruction in aerial combat of 20 and a half enemy aircraft.

He returned to Australia at the end of 1942 and was subsequently posted as Wing Leader of No 1 Fighter Wing where by his confidence, coolness, the skill and determination of his leadership in the air and the offensive spirit he displays at all times he has set a most excellent example to all pilots of the Wing.

His skill and judgment as a leader are outstanding.

On March 2nd 1943 he led a formation of six Spitfires against more than double the number of the enemy, personally shooting down and destroying two of them. On numerous occasions since then he has led the Wing of 36 and 48 Spitfires against large numbers of enemy raiders with great success and personally destroyed three more enemy aircraft.

W/Cdr Caldwell has carried out over 300 operational sorties against the enemy in various theatres of war and in doing so has flown over 475 active operational flying hours.

His personal score of enemy aircraft destroyed in aerial combat has now passed 25, five of which are Japanese and shot down since his return to Australia.

His personal courage, determination and skill and his

undoubtedly outstanding ability as a leader are an inspiration to all ranks and worthy of the highest praise.

RECORD OF SERVICE EXTRACTS FROM THE OFFICIAL FLYING LOG BOOK OF GROUP CAPTAIN CR CALDWELL
ASSESSMENTS made by Commanding Officers

5.9.41 by Squadron Leader JE Scoular DFC Commanding No 250 (Fighter) Squadron RAF Middle East:

An extraordinarily keen fighter pilot who is apt to let his keeness get the better of him. Needs more practice in leading, and will turn out a very good pilot. At the moment he is purely an individualist.

30.12.41 by Wing Commander EJ Morris DSO Wing Leader of No 238 (Fighter) Wing RAF:

An exceptional fighter pilot whose leadership and skill in combat have been of the highest order.

8.5.1942 by Air Chief Marshal Sir Arthur Tedder, Air Officer Commanding-in-Chief RAF Middle East Command:

A fine commander, an excellent leader and a first class shot

23.6.1943 by Group Captain Walters, AFC Commanding No1 Fighter Wing RAAF:

While serving under my command Wing Commander Caldwell has demonstrated outstanding ability as Wing Leader and individually as a fighter pilot. He has at present over 25 confirmed victories to his credit.

17.1.46 Opinion by Air Commodore AH Cobby DSO, DFC Air Officer Commanding Tactical Air Force RAAF:

While serving under me Group Captain Caldwell's operational services were outstanding. His administrative ability was exceptional. His Wing was very efficient and well organised.

Combat Claims

KILL	DATE	TYPE	RESULT	LOCALITY
1.	26 June 1941	Bf 11	Destroyed	Fort Cappuzo, Egypt
2.	30 June 1941	Bf 110	Destroyed (shared)	off Tobruk, Libya
3	30 June 1941	Ju-87	Destroyed	off Tobruk
4.	30 June 1941	Ju 87	Destroyed	off Tobruk
5.	7 July 1941	Fiat G 50	Destroyed	Gazala, Libya
6.	16 Aug 1941	Fiat G 50	Destroyed (shared)	Convoy patrol
7.	29 Aug 1941	Bf 109F	Destroyed	Sidi Barrani, Egypt
8.	27 Sept 1941	Bf 109	Destroyed	BuqBuq, Egypt
9.	28 Sept 1941	Bf 109	Destroyed	Bardia, Libya
10.	23 Nov 1941	Bf 109	Destroyed	off Tobruk
11.	23 Nov 1941	Bf 109	Destroyed	Beir el-Baheira, Libya
12.	5 Dec 1941	Ju 87	Destroyed	South of El Adem, Libya
13.	5 Dec 1941	Ju 87	Destroyed	South of El Adem
14.	5 Dec 1941	Ju 87	Destroyed	South of El Adem
15.	5 Dec 1941	Ju 87	Destroyed	South of El Adem
16.	5 Dec 1941	Ju 87	Destroyed	South of El Adem
17.	12 Dec 1941	Bf 109	Destroyed	Derna-Tmimi, Libya
18.	20 Dec 1941	Bf 109	Destroyed	S. Barce, Libya
19.	24 Dec 1941	Bf 109	Destroyed	Derna-Gazala, Libya
20.	14 Mar 1942	Macchi-Castoldi 202	Destroyed	NW Tobruk
21.	14 Mar 1942	Macchi-Castoldi 202	Destroyed (shared)	NW Tobruk
22.	23 Apr 1941	Bf 109	Destroyed	Bir Hacheim, Libya
23.	2 Mar 1943	Nakajima B 5N Kate	Destroyed	Pt Charles, Australia
24.	2 Mar 1943	Mitsubishi A 6M Zero	Destroyed	Pt Charles, Aust
25.	2 May 1943	Mitsubishi A 6M Zero	Destroyed	NW Darwin
26.	20 June 1943	Mitsubishi A 6M Zero	Destroyed	NW Darwin
27.	30 June 1943	Mitsubishi A 6M Zero	Destroyed	SW Darwin
28.	30 June 1943	Mitsubishi G 4M Betty	Destroyed	65km W Batchelor
29.	30 June 1943	Mitsubishi G 4M Betty	Destroyed	65 km W Batchelor
30.	20 Aug 1943	Mitsubishi Ki 46 Dinah	Destroyed	W Cape Fourcroy

To this total of 30 (27 and three shared destroyed) must be added six probables and fifteen damaged. Caldwell accounted for ten Me-109s.

Acknowledgements

Thanks for much assistance and permission to use material are due to: Jim Grant, Jean Caldwell, Bruce Watson, Bobby Gibbes, Ted Sly, Graham Masters, Dick Cresswell, Peter Radtke; and the very helpful staff at the National Library of Australia, the National Archives of Australia, and the Australian War Memorial.

In addition, the following books were most helpful:

Aces High: Chris Shores and Clive Williams (Neville Spearman)
Fighters Over the Desert: Chris Shores and Clive Williams (Neville Spearman)
Darwin's Air War: Robert Alford (Colemans Printing Pty Ltd, Darwin)
Spitfires Over Darwin: Jim Grant
Test Pilot: Neville Duke (Grub Street Press)
You Only Live Once: Bobby Gibbes

Index

Clark, Flying Officer
  Tommy, 156
Clostermann, Pierre, 3
Cobby, Air Commodore
  Harry, 19, 180, 185, 187,
  188–9, 208, 210, 211, 219,
  220–5, 269
Collishaw, Raymond, 19
Commonwealth Aircraft
  Corporation, 10
Coningham, Arthur 'Maori',
  19, 72
Cooper, Sergeant, 120
Cowper, Andrew King, 19
Cresswell, Wing
  Commander Dick, 23,
  101, 162, 214–15, 219, 260
Cross, Group Captain, 85
Crystal, Bill, 174
Curtiss aeroplanes, 96
Curtiss C 46 Commando,
  98–9

Darwin, 109–68
David, Fred, 102
Davoren, Flight Lieutenant
  John, 231
De La Rue, Air
  Commodore, 209

Deere, Al, 3, 104
deflection shooting, 37–42,
  123, 170–2
Dempster, Paddy, 197
Derma, Sergeant, 71
Dixon, Squadron Leader,
  217
Drakeford, Air Minister, 208
Duigan, John, 17
Duke, Neville, 3, 33, 48,
  66–7, 72, 74–6, 82, 83–4,
  88
Duncan, Flight Sergeant
  Colin, 157–9

Eguchi, Lieutenant Akira,
  122
Elliott, Sergeant, 71

Falkiner, George, 242–3,
  250
Fiat CR 42 Falco (Falcon),
  46, 47, 48
Fiat G 50 Freccia (Arrow),
  47, 58, 61
fighter pilots
  age restrictions, 20–2
  Australian, 14–16
  characteristics, 14–16

Also by Jeffrey Watson

SIDNEY COTTON – THE LAST PLANE OUT OF BERLIN

Sidney Cotton was a superb pilot, a talented inventor, a businessman who was decidedly shady—and a spy.

Born in Queensland, he served as a pilot in World War I, and over the next twenty years did everything from delivering mail in Newfoundland to entering the world of aerial reconnaissance on behalf of MI6, making numerous spy flights over Germany and Italy.

For a time he had the direct support of Churchill, but fell out with the authorities because of his unorthodox style— which included accepting money to fly businessmen out of Paris as it fell. . .

He ran guns in India after partition, and led the high life— but in the end died bankrupt after oil exploration in Saudi Arabia went wrong.

'a remarkable Australian who combined the elements of Biggles, James Bond and Oscar Schindler.'

SUNDAY LIFE

'the tale of a true soldier of fortune, who left his mark wherever he walked or flew or sailed. . .'

CANBERRA TIMES